# A TASTE OF SCOTLAND'S ISLANDS

## SUE LAWRENCE

is a food writer and journalist who has written many books on cooking and baking, including *The Scottish Kitchen* (2002), *The Sue Lawrence Book of Baking* (2004), *Eating In* (2011) *Scottish Baking* (2014), *The Scottish Berries Bible* (2015) and *The Scottish Soup Bible* (2017). Born in Dundee, she was brought up and educated in Edinburgh, then at Dundee University and later working as a journalist with D.C. Thomson. She was the winner of *MasterChef* (BBC TV) in 1991. President of the Guild of Food Writers from 2004 to 2008, she has received many awards, including a Glenfiddich Award in 2003. She lives in Edinburgh.

# A TASTE OF
# Scotland's
# Islands

## SUE LAWRENCE

*Enjoy the Islands!*
*Best wishes,*

**BIRLINN**

*Sue Lawrence*

First published in 2019 by Birlinn Ltd
West Newington House
10 Newington Road
Edinburgh
EH9 1QS
www.birlinn.co.uk

Design and layout by James Hutcheson and Tom Johnstone

ISBN: 978-1-78027-600-7

British Library Cataloguing in Publication Data
A catalogue record for this book is available from the British Library

Typeset in Adobe Garamond Pro at Birlinn

Printed and bound by PNB, Latvia

*Photo opposite title page: South Lochs, Lewis.*

# CONTENTS

For Matilda and Harris,
with love
The world's your oyster

ACKNOWLEDGEMENTS

Thank you to Jamie Logan and Mike Plews for your wonderful professional food photos; you'll go far, a brilliant team! And thanks to 'Life Story', the Scandinavian design-led store in Edinburgh, for lending us their beautiful tableware for the shoot (www.lifestoryshop.com).

Thanks to the following islanders (and those with strong island connections) who, along with the wonderful people mentioned in the book, helped me find the very best cooks and ingredients; they have also often fed me delicious island fare: Christine Bryden, Maggie Darling, Ronnie Eunson, John Gordon, Emma and Ron Goudie, Helen and Ian Gray, Isabel and Martin Johnson, Bea and Donnie MacDonald, Shona MacIntyre, Iain MacLeod, Sally Swinbanks, Hamish Taylor, Mary and Martin Whitmore.

Thanks to the following for so kindly giving their photos for use in the book: Fiona Bird (pages 31 and 44), Ria Macdonald (pages 2, 47, 58, 121, 123 and 134) and John J. MacLennan (page 187).

Thanks also to my brilliant agent, Jenny Brown, whose sunny disposition, proficiency and perseverance make her the very best agent to have.

And thank you to all the excellent team at Birlinn for believing in this book.

# Introduction

I have always been drawn to the islands. Ever since we went on family picnics over the causeway to Cramond Island in the Firth of Forth when my children were small, I was hooked. The walk over the mile-long stone causeway beside the anti-boat pylons constructed in the Second World War was always timed precisely – well, as precisely as possible with three small children – as access is restricted by tidal flow. There is some six to seven hours between low tide and high tide, and so we would allow for having no more than four hours over on the island. Many are the tales of people being stranded and having to be rescued by RNLI. We have stood on the shore trying not to look smug, having read the Tides Notices and Warnings, as shamefaced day-trippers disembarked from the lifeboats called out to rescue them as the high tide engulfed the causeway.

We used to make bonfires on the beach, cook sausages and then ram marshmallows onto green sticks to char until black. Tongues would be burnt as the wait to get started on the hot gooey mallow was always too much for little ones. Of course the history of Cramond Island always interested me more than it did my children, who were more keen on running around the small island, free as birds. That's the good thing about a small island; there was no danger of getting lost.

Cramond Island was used in the past for sheep-farming and before overfishing virtually wiped out molluscs in the Forth, there were also oyster beds. During the Second World War, the island was fortified and the anti-boat barrier was put in place to prevent submarines reaching Rosyth Dockyard.

I love the story of King James IV's linguistic experiment on an island near Cramond Island, Inchkeith (though some say it was on neighbouring Inchmickery). In the late fifteenth century, the Scottish monarch, keen to discover whether human language was in fact divinely inspired, sent a mute woman to look after two newborn infants on the uninhabited island for several years. Some accounts – those wishing to flatter the king – said the children could speak Hebrew (naturally assumed to be 'the language of God'); others said they could merely gesticulate and had no words at all. Only on an island could that atrocious experiment have taken place and the very thought of its seclusion and isolation is both exciting and terrifying.

*The Causeway to Cramond Island.*

Another Firth of Forth island, the Isle of May, has been revealed as a centre for early medieval medicine. Archaeologists found graves whose occupants had suffered serious diseases. Researchers are convinced the sick went there to be healed, since traces of medicinal plants such as greater celandine, used for pain relief, and henbane, which acted as an anaesthetic, have been found.

It was in the now uninhabited Monach Islands, to the west of North Uist, that Lady Grange was held a prisoner for two years from 1732, having been kidnapped and taken there on the orders of her husband, Lord Grange, who was Lord Chief Justice in Edinburgh. After she had managed to escape from there, she was then taken to even remoter St Kilda. A further six years of misery followed, until when there was yet another possibility of her escaping she was removed finally to Skye where she died, a tragic and misunderstood victim. Each island has its own story to tell.

When my children were older, holidays were spent on the islands of Islay, Lewis and Harris. Here we had ferries to take us over from the mainland and we weren't subject to the vagaries of the tides. These were bigger places where the children could not run wild as they had done on Cramond Island, and yet there was still a safe freedom. They were far more remote islands but they still had that magic.

On our first visit to Islay, again I found the history fascinating. Loch Finlaggan on Islay was formerly the administrative centre of the Lords of the Isles who controlled the whole of the Western Isles and beyond. Written records for Islay are older than for any other Hebridean island and archaeological digs have found pre-fourteenth century sites both at Eilean Mor, the main island in Loch Finlaggan, and also on Eilean na Comhairle, the crannog joined by a causeway to Eilean Mor. On both of these islands are ruins of houses, a great hall, burial ground and chapel. While I was desperate to visit all the ruins, my children simply wanted to play on the beach. For we had happened upon Islay in a heatwave – in May – which was unbelievable. Every day, we trundled buckets and spades through the high dunes down onto the white sandy beaches and paddled with the children, then picnicked on the dunes while watching the black or chocolate-coloured cows stroll along the sand. Some days we were lucky enough to chat to a fisherman who would sell us a couple of crabs, and I would boil these back at the house and teach the kids how to crack the claws and suck out the delicious sweet meat. Fortunately all meals were taken outside during that improbably hot May as this was a very messy business.

This was in the early 1990s, when very few crabs, lobsters or langoustines were retained in Scotland; rather, they were packed immediately into vivier trucks and taken to France and Spain, while the shellfish that had for centuries been part of every Hebridean islander's diet was now superseded on the islands by processed meats and frozen fish fingers. And so the seafood was sent, frozen and chilled, to Paris and Madrid to be enjoyed by diners who marvelled at their quality.

The next island family holiday was to Lewis. We went in July. This will be a repeat of Islay in the heatwave, we all thought as we left Edinburgh in a drizzle and drove north to Ullapool for the ferry. One week later, the rain had eventually stopped and we were able to recognise something called blue sky as we disembarked from the ferry at Ullapool back from Stornoway. It happens, of course, everywhere, but for this type of outdoor holiday with our three children we needed it to be dry for at least one day; now they were in their early teens, the prospect of taking a long walk in the rain ('It'll be fun!') appalled them. But this was the holiday that their love of fishing began. My husband would drag them all reluctantly along to the nearby tiny harbour, rods in hand. They returned with a couple of mackerel which were promptly gutted and cooked for tea – fresh and delicious. And on yet another rainy day we all headed across moors and peat bogs to a lochan where they fished for brown trout. Again, another simple teatime treat. Our recollections of holidays on the Scottish islands don't have to be bathed in sun and cloudless skies – even in mist and continuous drizzle, huddled under windbreaks or enveloped in waterproofs – memories were made. I have also been to Orkney, Shetland, Mull, Arran, Tiree and Harris when the beaches have resembled the Caribbean – but without the crowds. There is no doubt the beaches on the Scottish islands are some of the finest in the world. You don't come to the islands for the weather; but when you get it, what a bonus.

What you come for nowadays, more and more, is the food. Decades ago, the food eaten on the islands was almost all local. Apart from tea, coffee and sugar, most other ingredients were taken from the field outside the croft or the sea at your doorstep. Salting and then smoking both fish and meat were traditional methods of preserving food before refrigeration; and of course fruits were bottled and preserved to last the winter. With the introduction of refrigeration and the ease of air transport, though, the muddling of the seasons began. Instead of waiting for that first raspberry to emerge from between the canes at the foot of the garden, you could find berries imported from far afield. Instead of awaiting the new lamb season, there were imports of frozen lamb from the other side of the world. And with this gradual change came a shift in attitude. Instead of treating crabs and oysters as everyday fare if you lived near the sea, because there was little else to eat, they became the food of the elite or were immediately shipped off to the continent where they were devoured appreciatively. Instead of cooking an old-fashioned plate of mince, tatties and skirlie, islanders, like the rest of Scots on the mainland, would return from foreign holidays and cook spaghetti Bolognese or chilli con carne. Nothing wrong with that, obviously; variety is never a bad thing. And the choice now on the islands is so much better than it was in the 70s and 80s when you were often lucky to find any fresh fruit in a local shop. But sometimes it felt as if the food of the islands had lost its link with the past. Just as Gaelic was being heard less frequently, so traditional dishes were cooked less

*Beach at the head of Lochindaal, Islay,*

*Langoustines, Islay.*

often. Even now, as the older generations pass on, so many of the old dishes and recipes die. Not all, of course, are worth reviving, but the core ethos – that local and seasonal is always best – is most definitely good.

But there is now certainly hope. On my tour of the Scottish islands, I was fortunate to speak to many producers and cooks who continue to use local ingredients; some still use traditional recipes, perhaps brought a little up to date to suit modern palates. On the beautiful island of Raasay, the village shop in Inverarish is flourishing, selling everything from Skye's Misty Isle Gin (accompanied by the shopkeeper's tasting notes – 'you get a hint of cinnamon') to postcards and ice-cream. They also sell local venison, and salad leaves, edible flowers and vegetables from the walled garden at Raasay House. John William Gillies, the 'deer man', now adds red wine, red pepper and Worcestershire sauce to his traditional venison casserole. Dulse or another frond of seaweed from the shore is added to an island gin along with tonic. Modern ideas combined with traditional ingredients is surely the way ahead, but always with a respect for the past.

On the remote island of Scalpay, there is one of the best seafood restaurants in the Outer Hebrides and diners flock to the bistro doors to taste the chef's local shellfish. Scalpay, which only had its connecting bridge to Harris built in the 1990s, now has a flourishing population. And though the large school no longer educates the island children (they now have to travel to Tarbert for schooling), the school buildings have become a wonderful art and craft 'village', with enterprising people making full use of the space to make tweed, linen, paintings and gifts using driftwood from the shores. One of the crafts people makes table lamps using the up-cyclable Harris gin bottles.

On the island of Great Bernera, the population, which was dwindling before the bridge was built in the 1950s, has increased a little, with incomers appreciating the beauty of the islands; and now easier accessibility and better infrastructure help. The café and museum there draw islanders in to find out about their heritage and local history – as well as to enjoy a cup of tea and slab of excellent home-baked cake.

On the island of Jura, there is a wonderfully enterprising set-up on one of the beaches: the teenage children of the three Jura gin distillers bake delicious cakes and provide these for summer visitors to the beach, with an honesty box in place for donations.

Visiting the Scottish islands has always been, to me, a joy, whatever the weather. But with more focus on local sourcing in restaurants and cafés, more availability of local ingredients in shops and of course more artisan food producers and farmers' or producers' markets, they are now also a culinary cornucopia. And provided we respect both history and nature, visitors will surely continue to be welcome. Island life is alive and well and the distance it takes to get to some of them should never be an obstacle; it is all part of the adventure.

Robert Louis Stevenson's famous quote: 'To travel hopefully is a better thing than to arrive' used to ring true in island holidays of the past when the arrival heralded a week of mostly canned or processed food. Now the journey is easier with faster ferries and flights, though these are still weather-dependent: my trip to Shetland for this book was delayed both going and returning for hours by fog in the middle of a sunny May. There are also more connecting bridges: Skye is not even classified as an island now in some books because of its long bridge from the mainland.

But as well as improved infrastructure, the welcome on the table is now more likely to be an abundance of local produce and the cuisine both modern and traditional. This book is my personal culinary tour, a discovery of wonderful cooking on some of Scotland's many idyllic islands. It is partly my tribute to the wild beauty of the islands and to their people; mostly, however, it is a celebration of their food.

*Vidlin Voe, Shetland.*

*Opposite: Cranberry and Orange Bere Muffin (Orkney).*

# I
# Breakfast
# Bakes

# SHETLAND BANNOCKS
*makes 10–12*

*Isabel and Martin Johnson are excellent Shetland hosts. During my last visit to Lerwick, we had breakfast in the garden; by 11 am, the thermometer was registering an astonishing 34C, almost unheard of in the month of May. But what made this breakfast outside in the garden with a view over to the island of Bressay, was the bannocks. Isabel's recipe, from her home town of Vidlin in the north east of the mainland, is usually made by Martin who insists they are quick to rustle up early in the morning. In different places in Shetland, they are sometimes called scones or floury bannocks, but in Vidlin Isabel knew them just as bannocks. They are also sometimes baked on a girdle, instead of in the oven. At the traditional Shetland teas – served in church halls on Sundays and at weddings, funerals and Up Helly-Aa, these would always be served, often with local butter and that island staple, rhubarb jam. But because they have no sugar, they are also delicious served with soup; I especially enjoy them with Reestit Mutton soup.*

| | |
|---|---|
| 225g self-raising flour | 40g butter, diced |
| 1 tsp baking powder | 150ml buttermilk |
| ½ tsp cream of tartar | |

Sift the first three ingredients into a bowl with a pinch of salt, and rub in the butter.

Mix 50ml of cold water into the buttermilk and then slowly add this to the bowl, mixing gently with a table knife, to combine to a soft dough. You might need another 10ml or so of water.

Gently pat out on a floured surface, cut into squares or triangles and place on a greased baking sheet. Bake at 220C/425F/Gas 7 for about 10 minutes before removing to a wire rack. Eat warm with butter.

# Beremeal
## (Orkney mainland)

I can think of few places in the world where there is such evidence of the continuity of diet spanning 5,000 years. But on Orkney, the collective name for the archipelago of 70 islands off the north east of Scotland, I was lucky enough to visit the fascinating Skara Brae, a Neolithic village dating back to 3,100 BC, centuries before the Pyramids of Giza were built. At Skara Brae, the best-preserved Neolithic village in Europe, you can look inside the houses from the Middle Stone Age with their central fire and a large stone, to cook their bread or bannocks on, at the side; you can see the 'saddle querns' where barley was ground between two stones. Neolithic Orcadians ate – as well as seabirds such as fulmars, gannets and auks – shellfish, fish, cheese, meat and game. And barley. Wheat was also found in excavations here, which is interesting as it is no longer possible for it to be grown as it is too cold; Orkney 5,000 years ago was some three degrees warmer than now.

This diet pretty much reflects the diet nowadays, apart from the seabirds, but the interesting continuous feature of this diet to me is barley. This would have been the ancient variety of barley known as bere which has been grown since Neolithic times on these islands. Nowadays, although it has become rather rare following the gradual change to the more commercial types of barley used primarily on Orkney for cattle feed, bere-growing and milling is still very much alive and well on Orkney.

So it was I headed north on the mainland, to the Barony Mills at Birsay, which were built in 1873. In those days there were dozens of watermills all over the islands. The saddle querns of Neolithic times had given way to trough querns in the Bronze Age, then to rotary querns in the Iron Age and finally to the more sophisticated water-powered wheel, introduced by the Norsemen, to grind the grain. By the end of the seventeenth century there were at least 50 mills in Orkney; nowadays there is just one working mill – the one at Birsay.

I entered this tall Victorian mill on a bitterly cold day, the wind whipping outside against the weather-worn stone. The miller then was Rae Philips, whose father and grandfather had also been millers here, and Rae showed me what constitutes his working day during the long winter months: milling bere. In the summer, the mill becomes a tourist attraction. Rae has since passed away, but his legacy lives on.

The bere, formerly known by its Norse name of *bygg*, arrives at the mill and is dried down for six to eight hours to a moisture level of about 8 to 10%, ready for grinding. Then

*The Bay of Meil near Kirkness, Orkney.*

the great wheel outside the mill creaks into action as the sluice gates are opened and the enormous weight of water causes the wheel to slowly turn. The dried grain is then taken to the stones: firstly the shelling stones, to crack the husk and free the kernel. The husks are not wasted but are used to heat the kiln. Secondly the kernels are delivered to a pair of French 'burr' stones to be ground into coarse meal called grap. This unsieved, roughly ground bere is then reground to a fine meal by the bere stones, which also remove the dust. This bere flour or meal is sieved and bagged for customers to make into bannocks, oatcakes and pancakes – a taste of the past worth preserving.

# Bere Bannocks

*makes 1 bannock, to be divided into 4 pieces*

*This is my adaptation of a recipe from Paul Doull of the wonderful Foveran Hotel near Kirkwall. Paul taught me how to make these bannocks one chilly February morning. Having taken the whole morning off to see the maestro in action, I could hardly believe it when they were ready, a mere fifteen minutes later. There they were on the wire rack, covered with a tea towel to keep them moist: four of the most beautiful bannocks, speckled all over with charred marks. They were so quick to make, that gave me more time to enjoy them with Orkney butter and coffee while looking out from the Foveran's dining-room window to the glorious vista of Scapa Flow and the islands beyond.*

75g beremeal

75g self-raising flour

1 level tsp bicarbonate of soda

1 rounded tsp cream of tartar

½ tbsp vegetable oil

First put a girdle or solid frying pan on to heat to a steady heat: this can take a good 10 minutes. Very lightly oil the surface.

Mix the flours, soda, tartar and a ¼ tsp of salt in a bowl. Make a well in the middle and add the oil, then enough cold water to combine to a soft dough (about 150ml). Tip onto a board dusted with a little beremeal and shape gently into a bannock shape: a round about 15–17cm diameter and about 2–2.5cm thick (it puffs up as it cooks). Use a very light touch and do not knead.

Slap it onto the girdle and cook, without poking or touching, for 5 minutes, then turn and continue to cook for 4 minutes. Both top and bottom will be scorched all over and golden brown. Remove and place on a wire rack, loosely covering with a tea towel to keep the top soft. Tempting though it is to devour them hot, leave until cold before splitting open and spreading with butter. Classically served with oily fish such as herring or Orkney cheese, they are also excellent with anchovies or fish pâté.

# CRANBERRY AND ORANGE BERE MUFFINS

*makes 8 large muffins*

*My recipe is based on one from Lorraine at Cafelolz, Kirkwall, Orkney. Lorraine Pilkington-Tait, also known as Lol, hence the café name, was born and bred in Stenness on the mainland of Orkney, then worked for in the hospitality industry all over Scotland. She is a self-taught baker and cook and opened Cafelolz in 2000. Before that she lived in New Zealand for 15 years with her Kiwi husband, and it was there she embraced the wonderful coffee/café culture of NZ. Lorraine's bestsellers in the café include gluten-free brownies and, of course, her legendary Orkney Fudge Cheesecake.*

100g beremeal

100g self-raising flour

50g dark brown muscovado sugar

75g caster sugar

1 level tsp bicarbonate of soda

1 level tsp cinnamon

100g dried cranberries

the zest and juice of one small orange (50ml juice)

100g butter, melted and cooled slightly

2 large eggs

5 heaped tbsp natural yoghurt

25g–40g sunflower and/or pumpkin seeds

Mix the beremeal, flour, sugars, bicarbonate and cinnamon together in a large bowl. Stir the cranberries through. Sprinkle over a few of the seeds.

In a separate bowl, combine the orange juice and zest with the butter, eggs and yoghurt. Gently combine the two bowls; do not over-mix.

Dollop spoonfuls into 8 large muffin cases in a bun tin, then sprinkle the remaining seeds on top.

Bake in a preheated oven (200C/400F/Gas 6) for 10 minutes, then reduce to 180C/350F/Gas 4) for a further 15 minutes or so, until a wooden cocktail stick inserted into the centre comes out dry. Baking time is about 25 minutes altogether.

Eat warm, with a dod of butter if required.

*Cranberry and Orange Bere Muffin.*

# Luing Sourdough Bread
## (Isle of Luing)

Luing sourdough uses grains that used to be grown on Luing, primarily barley and oats with a small amount of rye. In 1549 Luing was said to be 'guid for corn', and in 1772 Thomas Pennant described the island as 'almost entirely covered with excellent corn'. The word 'corn' historically denotes oats and barley, sometimes also rye. Until the eighteenth century, rent payments by tenants included quantities of bere (barley) and meal (oatmeal). For centuries rye was grown in small quantities in the Hebrides, often together with oats and barley as mixed crops. Bannocks of barleymeal, oatmeal or 'mashlam', a combination of grains, were once a staple food of the islanders. Though nowadays most of the land on Luing is cattle and sheep grazing, the gentle slopes and low-lying landscape would then have been covered with corn – whether oats or barley or rye – all through the summer months.

In this delicious bread, whole flakes of barley, jumbo oats and rye are soaked for several hours before mixing the dough. The resulting loaf is moist and flavoursome, and keeps very well. The recipe is from talented Luing island baker Mary Braithwaite, who runs the island bakery. Mary, an archaeologist by profession, and husband Nigel, moved to Luing in 2015. Previously they had set up and run a village bakery in Wye, Kent, but were keen to escape the bustle of life in southern England and scale down their baking activities. They first had the idea of opening a bakery when they moved back to the UK in 2007 after decades abroad and were unable to find good bread. They did some training with Andrew Whitley, UK guru of real bread, and then with the French National Bakery Institute (INBP) in Rouen, France, where they learnt the methods and techniques they use today. Their breads use slow processes and 'pre-ferments', which make the bread tasty, digestible and long-keeping. Mary buys her organic flour from Mungoswells Millers in East Lothian.

Since moving to Luing and a less frantic lifestyle, Mary has developed breads for her bakery using grains that were once grown on Luing, especially barley and oats. Other breads include rye, spelt and Orkney beremeal.

She won two Gold Medals and two Bronze at the Royal Highland Show in 2017 and 2018: in the 'Traditional and Ancient' category, she won with her 'Clootie Loaf', an enriched sweet loaf similar in flavour to a cloutie dumpling, made with dried fruit, apple, molasses and spices. She won another category – 'Bread excelling in nutritional quality' –with her toasted seed and oat sourdough, containing golden flax and sunflower seeds.

# LUING SOURDOUGH

*makes 4 x 500g loaves*

*(they freeze well if you only need one small loaf)*

*Mary stipulates making the 'sponge' for this excellent loaf the night before. To make an overnight sponge, in a large bowl whisk together 190ml of water, 190g of white bread flour and ¼ tsp of active dried yeast until smooth. Cover and leave overnight in a cool place. It should froth up and double in volume, and smell sweet and yeasty when ready.*

*She suggests that regular bread bakers who have leaven to hand can use a liquid leaven (50% flour, 50% water) instead of the sponge described here.*

*Advance preparations: prepare the overnight sponge. Pour 400ml of boiling water over the grains, cover and leave to soak overnight, or for at least four hours.*

| | |
|---|---|
| 7g sachet active dried yeast | 120g whole barley flakes |
| overnight sponge (as above) | 120g whole jumbo oats |
| 600g strong white bread flour | 85g whole rye flakes |
| 175g strong wholewheat bread flour | |

For the dough, dissolve the dried yeast in 400ml of tepid water, in the mixing bowl. Add the overnight sponge, white and wholewheat flours and 4 level tsp salt. In an electric mixer, mix gently for 3 minutes with a dough hook (or knead by hand) until all the ingredients are brought together, then add in the soaked whole grains. Increase the speed slightly and mix for a further 10 minutes. Add a little more tepid water if the dough feels too stiff. It should be soft, and because of the soaked grains will feel slightly stickier than a normal bread dough. Scrape the dough into an oiled container, large enough to allow the dough to double in size. Cover and allow to prove for one and a half hours, folding the dough gently every half hour (scoop the edges of the dough and fold into the centre).

Tip the dough onto a floured surface and cut into four pieces of equal weight. Lightly fold each piece and leave to rest for 5–10 minutes. Shape the dough as required. If using loaf tins, shape into a neat cylinder and place seam-side down in the oiled tin. Prove

*Luing island baker, Mary Braithwaite.*

for 30–40 minutes, depending on the ambient temperature, until not quite doubled in volume. A floured finger pressed gently into the dough should see the dough spring only very slowly back; if it springs back quickly it needs extra proving; if it stays indented with no spring back it is overproved.

Slash the loaves with a sharp blade or knife immediately before loading into the oven. Put an old loaf tin on the bottom shelf of the oven, and pour some boiling water into the tin as the loaves are put in the oven; the steam helps the texture of the crust. Bake in a pre-heated oven (230–240C/450–475F/Gas 8–9) for around 30 minutes. When baked, the loaves should sound hollow when tapped on the bottom.

# Waas Bakery, Shetland

The Waas bakery in Walls, to the north-west of mainland Shetland, was bought over by an enterprising American, Bruce Gilardi, in 2016. He had family roots to the isles dating back to the 1890s. He rebranded the bakery and introduced many new products, both contemporary and traditional. Bruce sadly died in 2018 but then his legacy lived on, in the careful hands of head baker Gary Worrall, who was baking guru Dan Schickentanz's manager at the iconic Oxfordshire bakery, De Gustibus, which is often claimed to have been the original artisan bakery.

And so in the remote Shetland town of Walls is another exemplary artisan bakery with baker Gary in charge. The bestsellers are Tattie Braed (sic), with mashed potatoes incorporated into a butter-enriched dough, sourdough bread and Puckle Loaf made from granary flour and cracked wheat. (Puckle means a single grain of corn in Shetland dialect.)

*Ponies near Walls, Shetland.*

They also sell exquisite brownies, tiffin, American choc chip cookies, shortbread and oatcakes. They bake croissants, pains au chocolat and brioche for a French bistro in Lerwick, all made with local Shetland butter. And the Waas Bakery's 'Curnie Birl' is like a black bun but even nicer than the Scottish Hogmanay classic, as instead of shortcrust encasing the spiced currant filling, it has puff pastry.

To discover an artisan bakery anywhere is a joy; to find one in a small town some 35 miles north-west of Lerwick is little short of a miracle – don't forget bakery staff with their early morning starts (at 2 or 3 am) are not always easy to find. But it is thriving, with Waas bakery bread and other products sent all over the Shetland Islands, by car and ferry, to great acclaim. At the time of editing this book, baker Gary has left and Waas Bakery was up for sale, but thankfully still operational; here's hoping it continues to be a brilliant artisan bakery in the most northerly of the British Isles.

# PUCKLE BREAD
*Makes 2 loaves*

*This is my version of Waas Bakery's famous loaf.*

| | |
|---|---|
| 350g strong white bread flour | 75g cracked wheat |
| | one 7g sachet easy-blend yeast |
| 350g strong granary/malted grain flour | 2 tsp salt |

Mix the flours, wheat and yeast in a bowl with 2 level tsp of salt. Make a well in the centre and slowly pour in enough tepid water (about 450ml) to make a softish dough.

Using floured hands, bring the dough together and turn out onto a floured board then, regularly sprinkling (lightly) with flour (I use a flour shaker), knead for 10 minutes until smooth; it should be soft and shiny-looking but not too sticky.

Place in an oiled bowl, cover with clingfilm and leave somewhere warm for 1–2 hours to almost double in size (mine takes 2 hours to do this). Then punch down, divide into two and shape into 2 loaves. Place on 2 oiled baking sheets and cover with oiled clingfilm. Leave to rise again, somewhere warm, for about 45 minutes or until – when the dough is gently pressed with your finger – it does not spring back.

Slash the top lightly with a knife to form slits then dust lightly with flour and bake in a preheated oven (230C/450F/Gas 8) for 20–25 minutes or until the base sounds hollow when tapped.

# LEWIS OATCAKES
## *makes 24*

*This recipe is based on one from Anne Morrison, born and brought up in Ness, the town on the most northerly tip of Lewis. I spoke to her sister Marina Macdonald some years ago about her love for the local delicacy guga (baby gannet) and I recalled her telling me that it is the only time she ever drinks milk, when eating boiled guga and dry tatties.*

*Sister Anne is a great baker and bakes these delicious oatcakes often. I heard about them from her friend Rona who is one of the three Macleod women who run the award-winning Charles Macleod butchers in Stornoway. Rona used to bake them at home then tried them on a slightly larger scale in the butcher's. They became a great success and are baked a couple of times a week now for eager customers.*

*I reduced the sugar a little as I love them with savoury things – salted butter and a good farmhouse cheese, or some smoked mackerel pâté.*

| | |
|---|---|
| 175g butter, at room temperature | 150g self-raising flour |
| 35g light muscovado sugar | ½ tsp salt |
| 1 medium free-range egg | ½ tsp bicarbonate of soda |
| 250ml medium oatmeal plus extra for rolling | |

Beat the butter, sugar and egg together, then add the oatmeal, flour, salt and bicarbonate. Combine together gently with your hands (do not knead) and roll out on a board covered with a thin layer of oatmeal. You don't want to roll it too thin or the oatcakes will break up. Cut into about 24 rounds and place on a buttered baking sheet (you might need two) and bake at 160C/325F/Gas 3 for 20–25 minutes, until firm to the touch.

*The hills above Tarskavaig, Skye.*

*Opposite: Laver on beach at South Glendale, South Uist.*

# 2
# Soup, Vegetables, Seaweed

# Vegetables and Salads
## (Raasay)

Kate Smith is one of a team of two gardeners who now work the Raasay House Walled Garden after many years of neglect. The house itself has had an interesting history – built originally in the 1500s, it was burnt down by government troops after Culloden. Shortly after, in 1747, the building of the new Raasay House was begun, and in 1773, Dr Samuel Johnson and James Boswell stayed here as guests of the Macleod chief of Raasay. In his *Tour to the Hebrides*, James Boswell writes, 'The approach to Raasay was very pleasing. We saw before us a beautiful bay, well defended by a rocky coast; a good family mansion; a fine verdure about it, with a considerable number of trees; and beyond it the hills and mountains in gradation of wildness.'

In 2009, a massive fire destroyed the house again, just weeks before completion of the modern renovations, and so it had to be rebuilt again; it then opened as a hotel once more in 2013.

The Walled Garden was first mentioned in 1549 by Dean Munro, then by Martin Martin in 1695 as 'an orchard with several sorts of berries, pot herbs etc'. James Boswell described the garden in 1773 as being 'well stocked with kitchen stuff, gooseberries, raspberries, currants, strawberries, apple trees'. There are records of cherries, peas and strawberries being harvested in 1852, and indeed throughout the Victorian era the garden

*Raasay Walled Garden,* circa *1900.*

was renowned for its hothouses, peach houses and vineries. The garden had fallen into disuse over the years until it was decided in 2014 to run it as a community project, and the Walled Garden Action Group was formed.

Now there are two gardeners to tend the 1.4 acres and grow all sorts of vegetables, including carrots, courgettes, aubergines, sweetcorn, tomatoes, leeks, broad beans, peas, chillies, globe artichokes, pumpkin – and also herbs and many different types of salad leaves, including borage, nasturtium, mizuna, rocket, radish, oak-leaf lettuce, red and sweet basil and coriander. The produce is sold both to Raasay House where it is cooked and served in the restaurant, and the village shop where all islanders have a chance to buy this natural bounty. There is a compost toilet hut built in Raasay larch on entering the gardens and this somehow takes the visitor back a century or two to the days when everything was organic and natural as a matter of course.

Kate kindly gave me her recipe – using produce from the gardens and island potatoes – for a delicious vegetable soup with cheese. It is one of her children Ellie and Hamish's favourites.

# RAASAY WALLED GARDEN COURGETTE SOUP WITH CHEESE
### serves 4

*Kate likes to add a grating of nutmeg at the end; I prefer a handful of fresh mint leaves. The soup is made with unpeeled potatoes on the island, but I usually like to peel. So it's up to you; it all depends on the quality of the potato and the season.*

250g potatoes, washed, unpeeled or peeled, roughly chopped

1 organic vegetable stock cube

500g courgettes, roughly chopped

12 thin or 6 fat spring onions, trimmed, chopped

50g grated Cheddar (I like Isle of Mull cheese) plus extra, to serve

grating of fresh nutmeg or small handful of fresh mint leaves

Put the potatoes in saucepan with enough cold water to cover. Crumble in the stock cube and bring to the boil, cover and cook over medium high heat for 5 minutes, then add the courgettes. Cover again and cook for a further 5–7 minutes or until the vegetables are just tender. Throw in the spring onions and cook for a further 5 minutes, covered, then remove from the heat, add the nutmeg or mint and liquidise, adding salt and pepper to taste and a splash of boiling water if it requires thinning down.

Just before serving, add in the cheese, stir well until you have a molten goo then serve piping hot, with an extra scattering of grated cheese.

*Calum's Road, Raasay.*

# CLAPSHOT

*serves 4–6*

*This wonderful yet simple dish is from Orkney, and during a visit there I was lucky enough to try various versions. Sometimes the turnips are cooked in milk which makes it even creamier; but I advise you to use a very deep saucepan and keep the heat low once it has come to the boil otherwise the milk boils over easily. Sometimes a peeled, chopped onion is added to the potatoes as they cook for extra flavour. But this is the basic recipe, using plenty of good butter; Orkney's dairy produce is superb and the local butter, milk, cream and cheese abundant.*

*Elsewhere in the UK, it is easy for us to think a turnip is a turnip. Well, not on Orkney. There they are very particular about using winter neeps if possible, as they are drier and so the clapshot is not watery at all. Also, in order to have as much of the turnips' inherent sweetness, the best are those that have been in the ground through a hard frost. A final tip to make this dish truly Orcadian is to use a heavy hand with the pepper. Locals love it really peppery.*

*You can convert any leftovers into soup by thinning down with some good beef stock.*

500g potatoes, peeled (this is the peeled weight), cut up into chunks

500g turnip (swede), peeled (this is the peeled weight), cut up into chunks

75g butter

1–2 tbsp chopped chives, optional

Cook the vegetables in boiling water until tender, and drain; I bring them to the boil in cold salted water then boil, lid on, for 15–20 minutes, depending on size.

Return them to the pan, cover, then, over a very low heat, shake the pan to dry off completely. There must be no residual liquid. Mash with the butter and add salt and pepper to taste and the chives if using. Serve piping hot.

# REESTED MUTTON SOUP
*serves 6–8*

*Reested (reestit) mutton is a Shetland traditional dish of cured mutton, which has been salted for at least ten days, then hung up on hooks over a peat fire to dry for as long as it takes to be eaten up. After some time it looks rather like salt cod, with an ivory hue and a stiff cardboard feel. Some people have it hanging there for so long they wrap it around with newspapers to prevent the dust settling on it. The mutton is then sliced thinly – to Parma ham thinness – and fried with onions. Or – best of all – made into soup. No salt is added, yet it is perfectly seasoned with the cure of the meat, and the texture is thick and chunky with the vegetables. Traditionally eaten with slices of the cold reested mutton on the side, slices are also occasionally added to the soup just before serving.*

*Reested mutton was traditionally eaten during the winter months, originally as a means of preserving when there was little fresh meat, and is most readily available in butchers' shops in the run-up to Christmas. The flavour is so distinctive and unique, I believe it is well worth the long trek north to Shetland any day.*

*Since nowadays our palates are not as used to saltiness, I like to soak the mutton overnight in fresh water, throwing the water away the following day before making the soup.*

| | |
|---|---|
| 450g (approx) piece of reested mutton | 1 medium turnip (swede), peeled |
| 1 onion, peeled and chopped | 6–8 floury potatoes, peeled |
| 4–5 large carrots, peeled | |

Place the mutton in a large pan and cover with cold water. Bring to the boil and cook for about 30 minutes then chop all the vegetables into good-size chunks and add to the pan.

Return to the boil and cook, covered, until everything is tender – about 20 minutes. Remove the meat and cut off slices and put onto a plate. Serve piping hot, with the plate of sliced meat on the side.

*Lunna Kirk near Vidlin, Shetland.*

# Haggis, Neeps 'n' Tatties Soup

*serves 6*

*This recipe is from Kate MacDougall at the Harris Gin Distillery in Tarbert, where the most delicious soups are served every day. There is always a choice of two soups and this is one of the café customers' favourites.*

25g butter

2 large onions, peeled, roughly chopped

1 turnip (swede), peeled and chopped into chunks

5 large potatoes, peeled and chopped into chunks

2.5-3 litres vegetable stock

500g of haggis

1 dram of the finest whisky (Kate says ideally the Distillery's own Hearach Single Malt in a few years' time!) for drinking with this soup, optional

In a large pot, melt the butter and sweat off your onions until translucent. Add the turnip and cook for a further 5 minutes. Add your potatoes and vegetable stock and leave to boil until tender. Blend the soup, adding more stock or boiling water if needed, but the soup should remain quite thick for the haggis to sit on top of it.

Cube the haggis and fry off in a pan until crumbly in texture and cooked through. Spoon the soup into bowls and top with a generous scoop of haggis. Serve with fresh bread or oatcakes – and an optional dram!

# CORMORANT SOUP
*feeds many*

*Hamish Taylor from Flodaby on east Harris always used to make a cormorant casserole using the smaller cousin of the cormorant, the shag. He told me the shag has its 'season', i.e. autumn and winter, when the young have matured to independence of the parent bird and the parents have recovered condition after their summer breeding season and summer-spawned juvenile fish are in relative abundance for the bird to feed on.*

*He told me that since cormorants or shags eat only live fish, when skinned they are almost completely fat-free, and not at all oily or greasy; he insists they are not only wholesome and healthy, but also delicious. His recipe involves browning the floured cormorant or shag joints, adding onion, carrot, mushrooms and root vegetables, covering with boiling water and simmering until the meat is falling off the bone. He recommends a nice glass of Merlot to accompany.*

*This recipe below is more traditional, from* The Modern Crofters Cookbook *from the Museum of Great Bernera. It is reproduced in its original as I have a feeling not many readers will be off in search of a cormorant for the pot, and so it is more for historical interest. But if you do get a cormorant or shag, I advise you peel and chop the onions before adding to the pan!*

| | |
|---|---|
| 1 cormorant | 1 cup oatmeal |
| 6 pints water | 3 onions |

Clean the cormorant and cook in the water for 2 hours, adding the oatmeal and onions to make a soup of the stock.

Serve potatoes with the cormorant and eat the soup separately.

# ARDBEG SMOKED HADDOCK CHOWDER

*serves 3–4*

*Ardbeg Distillery was founded officially in 1815. 'Officially', as that was the date when the taxman discovered it, as the distillery is in a rather remote location on Islay! It is on the road east from Port Ellen, beyond Laphroaig and Lagavulin. Ardbeg also runs a most wonderful café restaurant in the old kiln, where the barley used to be malted. The chef, Andy Dyke, provides excellent fare, much of it using local ingredients. His smoked haddock chowder is fabulous – thick with fish and potatoes and with just the right amount of cream. Delicious.*

½ a medium onion, peeled and finely chopped

¼ fennel bulb, trimmed and finely chopped

½ a stick of celery, finely chopped

½ a small leek, cleaned and finely sliced

1 clove garlic, peeled and finely chopped

750g potatoes, peeled and diced (Andy likes to use Rooster)

knob of butter

1 litre fish stock

500g smoked haddock fillets, chopped

150 ml whipping cream

1 heaped tbsp parsley, chives and dill, chopped

zest and juice of half small lemon

Sweat the first six ingredients in a pan in the butter, stirring, for about 10 minutes until light golden. Add the stock and simmer till the potatoes are cooked, and add the smoked haddock and cream. Stir well, cook for 3–4 minutes until the fish is just cooked, then remove from the heat and add the herbs, lemon zest and juice. Check the seasoning and serve in warm bowls.

# SHIRLEY SPEAR'S BRAISED RED CABBAGE WITH BLUEBERRIES

*serves 6–8*

*This is the wonderful Shirley Spear's recipe for red cabbage with blueberries. Founder of the world-famous Three Chimneys at Colbost, Skye, she used to use local blueberries from Skye Berries at nearby Edinbane in the kitchen during their summer season. As well as using them in desserts, she incorporated them into this dish, which is delicious served with roast duck.*

6 juniper berries, crushed

8 whole cloves

½ cinnamon stick broken roughly into pieces

A piece of root ginger about the size of a brazil nut, sliced thinly

2 tsps soft dark brown sugar

Zest of half an orange

2 tbsp cider vinegar

Juice of 1 small orange

450g red cabbage, very thinly shredded

1 large onion, peeled and chopped small

1 large clove garlic, crushed

1 large cooking apple, peeled, cored and chopped small

25g butter

Whole nutmeg for grating

125g blueberries

Wrap the crushed juniper berries, whole cloves, broken cinnamon stick and sliced root ginger in a muslin square. Mix together the soft brown sugar with the orange zest. Mix together the cider vinegar and orange juice.

Put a layer of finely sliced red cabbage in a deep, ovenproof dish. Cover this with a layer of chopped onion, mixed with the crushed garlic and chopped apple, dot with butter. Season with salt, pepper and grated nutmeg. Sprinkle with the brown sugar and orange zest.

Bury the spices wrapped in muslin in this mixture, and cover with another layer of red cabbage. Season again with salt, pepper and a grating of nutmeg, then pour over the orange juice and cider vinegar. Dot with more butter.

*The Cuillin on Skye.*

Cover with a layer of greaseproof paper and either a close-fitting lid or a layer of foil. Place on a low shelf of a pre-heated oven (150C/300F/Gas 2) and cook slowly for up to 2 hours.

Remove the lid and greaseproof paper and stir the blueberries into the cooked cabbage mixture, cover and return to the oven and keep warm until serving. Just before serving, remove the muslin bag of spices and check the seasoning.

# Seaweed
## (South Uist)

'At the lowest tide, a wonderful ocean garden is revealed. For the savvy forager a delicious cornucopia of vegetables is ready for picking. Some seaweeds exist in the splash zone (as you go down to the beach) but many do not survive desiccation (the time that seaweeds aren't covered by water). Seaweeds adapt to the climate in which they grow. The seaside forager needs to make friends with the moon and tides to be in touch with the zone where each species grows. Spring is the time to discover seaweed. *Zone in. It's free.*' Thus speaks food writer and forager Fiona Bird, whose knowledge of seaweed in Scotland is second to none.

I first met Fiona years ago near her home in Angus when my three children – and her six – were small and so communication was always hurried. Recently, with more time at hand, however, I have come to read her eloquent ramblings on seaweed and foraging with interest – indeed fascination, for seaweed is something you have to understand and love. She is a woman with a passion.

Her husband Stephen is the local GP on South Uist, and since living on the Outer Hebrides she has become a regular visitor to the shores not far from her house. As well as using seaweed as a vegetable and adding to soups, scones and shortbread, she dries dulse and laver to add to bread recipes. For her excellent book *Seaweed in the Kitchen*, she has devised recipes such as seaweed brown bread ice-cream, dried seaweed biscuits and salmon laver and seville orange en croute.

Even I, a non-forager, can recognise such common seaweeds as dulse and kelp, the latter called tangle in Scotland – or cuvie depending on the species. Tangle and cuvie look similar: the stipe (stem) of tangle is very flexible and at low tide the tangle (*Laminaria digitata*) bends double. Meanwhile at low tide, cuvie (*Laminaria hyperborea*) stands to attention. Dulse often grows on cuvie, which has a rougher stipe. Other more familiar seaweeds are carragheen and sloke (called laver in Wales, nori in Japan). Fiona has many more on her list of daily seaweeds. These include the brown seaweed, sea spaghetti or thong weed (*Himanthalia elongata*), which, like sugar kelp, turns emerald green on cooking. The key to identifying sea spaghetti lies in its local name and its button, fungus-like base (holdfast) is helpful too.

Seaweed has been used for centuries on the Scottish islands. F. Marian McNeill in her 1929 *The Scots Kitchen*, writes that edible seaweeds found around the shores and islands

*Along the shore, South Uist.*

of Scotland include carragheen, tangle, bladderwrack, sloke and dulse. She mentions that on Barra it was used in Slokan, a dish of pulped dulse mixed with butter and served on a mound of mashed potatoes and often fried onions. McNeill writes that on Orkney, children eat the stems of some seaweeds raw, as they would stalks of rhubarb. And another Barra dish she mentions is the stalk from kelp roasted over peat fire embers and placed on a buttered barley bannock. Carragheen jelly is another hugely popular Hebridean dish, as it requires nothing but carragheen, milk and sugar – and perhaps some flavourings such as lemon, cinnamon or even rosewater.

Both cattle and sheep all around the Scottish islands roam along the shores and beaches freely, grazing on seaweed. This gives their meat a distinctive flavour and the Shetland lamb in particular has a wonderful savoury tang, which is often attributed to the sheep's seaside grazing.

Fiona Bird's foraging is always in harmony with nature, as she takes no more than she needs for a specific dish. She snips off the seaweed with scissors, leaving the rest to continue growing. Unlike plants, which have roots, the growing points of seaweeds vary. We have much to learn about harvesting sustainably, so the advice is to harvest sparingly, a little here and there.

Fiona advises rinsing the seaweed *in situ*; then it is essential to rinse thoroughly in several changes of fresh water when you return home to your kitchen. If you use a simple guide, there is a cornucopia of healthy goodness out there, just along the shore.

# ROOT AND SEA VEGETABLE SALAD

*serves 4*

*This is a recipe from Fiona and she says this is perfect for early spring. Sea spaghetti is also known as buttonweed due to its distinctive holdfast (by which it is attached to the rock); it is also known as thong weed. Early in the season this seaweed can be eaten raw from the rocks.*

*This wonderful recipe combines the earthy texture of winter celeriac with new growth sea spaghetti.*

400g fresh sea spaghetti

450g celeriac

Juice of half a small lemon

A large carrot

For the dressing:

2 tsp finely grated fresh ginger

2 tbsp rice vinegar

4 tbsp Greek yoghurt

2 tbsp toasted sesame seeds

4 tbsp olive oil

Cut the sea spaghetti into fork-easy lengths. Pop half of it into a colander and pour over a kettle of boiling water. It will turn green. Set aside to cool.

Peel the celeriac and cut it into match-sized pieces, no bigger. This is hard work: use a food processor if you are short of time, but the salad won't be as textured. Put the celeriac strips in a bowl, add the lemon juice and toss to coat (to prevent discolouration). Cut the carrot in a similar fashion and add to the prepared celeriac.

Make the dressing by blending the ginger, rice vinegar, yoghurt, seeds and a few twists of black pepper together. Whisk in the oil and pour over the prepared root vegetables. Toss well, season and add the green (blanched) and brown (raw) sea vegetables. Lightly mix the sea and root vegetables together and leave for ten minutes before serving.

# SEVILLE AND DULSE MARMALADE

*makes 5–6 jars*

*Fiona makes this unique-tasting marmalade using the whole fruit method and adding seaweed with the simmering oranges. The flavour of the seaweed impregnates the marmalade as it matures. She has also tried adding dried dulse at the rolling boil stage, but for a more intense flavour of the sea, she recommends following this recipe.*

3kg Seville oranges, well washed and stalks removed

Two large handfuls of roughly chopped, fresh dulse

Juice of a small lemon

3kg preserving sugar

Place the oranges and dulse in a jam pan. Cover with boiling water and cover the pan as best you can (I use a roasting tray). Simmer until the oranges are soft. This takes about two and a half hours.

When the oranges are cool, remove them from the cooking liquid. Measure the liquid. If there is more than 1.75 litres, reduce it by boiling rapidly. If there is less, make it up with additional water. The dulse will have softened and turned green. Chop up any larger pieces and return to the liquid.

Cut the Seville oranges in half and remove the seeds and flesh. A dessertspoon works well for this. Discard the pips and return the flesh to the pan. Cut the orange peel into pieces (thick or thin as desired) and add to the preserving pan with the juice of the lemon and the sugar. Return the jam pan to a low heat, stirring as the sugar dissolves.

When the sugar has dissolved, increase the heat and bring to a rolling boil. Continue to cook for 12 minutes or until the marmalade reaches setting point.*

Add a knob of butter to disperse any scum and leave to cool for 20 minutes. Ladle the marmalade into warm, sterile jam jars.

*Remove the pan from the heat when you test for a set.

*Opposite: Stornoway Harbour.*

# 3
# Fish

*Tobermory, Mull.*

# The Tobermory Fish Company
## (Mull)

The Tobermory Fish Company was founded in 1971 by Hugh and Marjorie Goldie in a shop in the main street of Tobermory, which has been an important fishing port since the late eighteenth century. The company is now run by their daughter Rosie Swinbanks and granddaughter Sally Swinbanks from their smokehouse overlooking Tobermory Bay at Baliscate. Here their famous smoked trout, salmon and haddock are sold and dispatched all over Scotland. The shop also sells local Mull produce such as Glengorm estate Highland beef and Mull haggis.

The salmon, which is farmed on the west coast including three Mull-based farms, is cold- and hot-smoked. Once filleted, the salmon is brined, seasoned (with a variety of flavourings form Cajun to marmalade) and hot-smoked for some 6 hours, then rested and packed. Their cold-smoked salmon is smoked at a very low temperature for 12 hours then, once chilled and rested, is hand-sliced by Rosie into long strips. The trout is smoked in a similar way and, along with the lightly smoked undyed smoked haddock, is hugely popular both on the island and on the mainland.

The smoked haddock is used in many ways, but one of the family's favourites is to have it in a Cullen Skink with Mull Cheddar croutons. The smoked salmon and trout are delicious not only as they are, with oatcakes or brown bread and butter and lemon, but also in dishes such as potato rosti with beetroot and horseradish and for topping blinis or scotch pancakes as canapes.

# Scotch Pancakes with Smoked Trout and Horseradish

*makes about 36 canape pancakes*

*This is my savoury Scotch pancake recipe, with the addition of chopped chives, which is Sally's brilliant idea. She likes to serve this with the Tobermory Fish Company's award-winning smoked trout, but smoked salmon is also good.*

125g self-raising flour, sifted

100g wholemeal self-raising flour

2 large free-range eggs

300ml milk

1 heaped tsp horseradish sauce

3 heaped tbsp finely chopped chives plus whole chives, to serve

Butter, for greasing

To serve:

300ml crème fraiche

2 tbsp horseradish sauce

300g cold-smoked trout (or salmon) slices

1 lemon, cut into wedges

Place the flours, eggs, milk and a pinch of salt in a food processor, add 1 tsp horseradish and the chives and process briefly until smooth. (Or whisk by hand with a balloon whisk.) If you have time, let the batter sit for ten minutes or so.

Place a large heavy-based frying pan or girdle on a medium heat and lightly butter the surface, using kitchen paper. When the pan is sufficiently hot (test by dropping a teaspoon of batter onto the surface: it should bubble within 1 minute) – drop 1 heaped tsp of batter onto the pan and repeat until you have covered the surface. After 1–2 minutes you will see bubbles, so that is the sign to flip over. Cook for a further 1 minute or so, until batter does not ooze out when lightly pressed with your fingers.

Remove to a wire rack and cover loosely with a tea towel. Continue making the pancakes until the batter is all used up. Once cool, lay the pancakes on a serving platter.

Mix the crème fraiche and horseradish, top each pancake with a small smear of the horseradish cream for the trout to stick, then add a nice ribbon of the smoked trout. Finish with a blob of the horseradish cream on top with some chives, a lemon wedge and some coarsely ground black pepper.

# HEBRIDEAN HOT-SMOKED SALMON FISHCAKES

*makes 4*

*These can be made in advance and frozen, either uncooked or cooked, then reheated in a medium oven till heated through. Salar Smokehouse on South Uist produces superb hot-smoked salmon.*

*You could also use cold-smoked salmon, snipped into small pieces. Try the smoked salmon from the Hebridean Smokehouse at Clachan on North Uist.*

*Serve with a green vegetable, a squeeze of lemon and perhaps a dollop of mayonnaise.*

1 large potato (weighing about 325g unpeeled), peeled and chopped

40g butter

Approx. 300g hot-smoked salmon

Grated zest and juice of 1 small lemon

2 tbsp finely chopped dill

1 small free-range egg, lightly beaten

1 heaped tbsp flour

4 heaped tbsp medium oatmeal

1 tbsp olive oil, to fry

Boil the potatoes till tender, then drain thoroughly and mash with the butter and plenty of salt and pepper to taste.

Flake in the salmon in large chunks then combine gently with the potatoes, adding the lemon juice, zest and dill. Check the seasoning.

Form into four fishcakes, chill well, then set out three plates out in a row. Put the egg in one, the flour in the next one and the oatmeal in the third. Dip each cake in egg, then flour, then oatmeal. Chill again.

Heat the oil in a shallow frying pan and, once hot, fry for 2 minutes on each side until golden, then place in heated oven (180C/350F/Gas 4) for about 20 minutes or until heated through.

# HOT-SMOKED TROUT
# POTATO GRATIN

*serves 4*

*Though I prefer using the plain hot-smoked trout from the Tobermory Fish Company, you can use their Cajun flavour too. Hot-smoked salmon from South Uist's Salar Smokehouse is equally good for this rich, creamy recipe. Serve with a green salad tossed in a light vinaigrette.*

| | |
|---|---|
| 1kg large waxy potatoes | 25g butter |
| 400g hot smoked trout, flaked | 2 tbsp wholegrain mustard |
| 300ml double cream | |

Peel the potatoes and cut into very thin slices (I slice in my food processor). Pat them dry on wads of kitchen paper.

Place half the potatoes in large buttered gratin dish, seasoning with plenty of freshly milled pepper and only a tiny grind of salt, as the salmon is salty. Place the salmon on top, cover with the rest of the potatoes and season again. Place the cream and butter in a pan and heat slowly, just until the butter melts, then remove from the heat and add the mustard. Pour this immediately over the dish – slowly – to ensure all the potatoes are covered.

Cover the dish with buttered foil and cook in a preheated oven (200C/400F/Gas 6) for 45 minutes, then remove the foil and continue to bake for a further 30 minutes or until the potatoes are completely tender. Allow to rest for at least 10 minutes before serving.

# SMOKED HADDOCK RAREBIT

*serves 2*

*This is a delicious brunch or supper dish. At brunch, serve simply with strong tea or coffee; at supper with a simple green salad and a glass of chilled white. There are many excellent fish-smokers all over the Hebrides and the Northern Isles; just ensure you use undyed.*

300g undyed smoked
   haddock fillets

250ml milk

25g butter

25g plain flour

1 level tbsp Dijon mustard

50g grated Mull Cheddar

2 English muffins split and
   lightly toasted

Place the fish in a saucepan with the milk. Bring slowly to the boil, bubble for 1 minute then remove from the heat and cover. Leave for half an hour or so, then strain through a sieve over a jug. Melt the butter in a saucepan, add the flour, stir for a minute and add the reserved fish liquor. Whisking, cook over a medium-low heat until smooth. Stir in the mustard, fish, cheese and seasoning to taste. Spread on top of the lightly toasted muffins and set on a grill tray. Grill until the topping is gooey and hot. Remove onto serving plates and serve at once, though a little patience is required: bear in mind hot molten cheese can burn your tongue!

## Crappit Heid and Ceann Cropaig; Krappit Muggie and Krappin (Hebrides; Shetland)

Some years ago, Lewis-born Rhoda MacLeod told me all about Crappit Heid, which she knew by the Gaelic name, Ceann Cropaig. (F. Marian McNeill called it 'piscatorial haggis'.)

In her soft Hebridean lilt she explained that first you need a very fresh fish. You must clean the liver thoroughly, then mash it with the oatmeal, using your hands, before stuffing into the head and boiling. She also used to steam the liver mixture in a bowl and discard the head. Rhoda made 'Marag iasg' (fish pudding) from the mashed-up liver (no oatmeal) too, and packed this into the cleaned fish gullet and boiled it, rather like a black or white pudding.

Rhoda often made sheep's head broth ('Ceann Caorach') by singeing the head, removing the eyes and splitting the head in half. After soaking in salt water overnight, it was rinsed and the brains smeared all over it (to remove the taste of singeing) and then boiled to make a fine broth with turnips, carrots, onion and barley. None of this, however, is for the faint-hearted.

The word Crappit Heid means stuffed head. Regional variations include 'Stappit Heidies' on mainland Scotland – in Caithness, Banff and Aberdeenshire. In Shetland, 'Krappin' is the stuffing that is either stuffed into a fish head or into a fish stomach (a 'muggie') to become Krappit Muggie. There are records of fishermen a few decades ago taking fish-liver and oatcake sandwiches to sea as their 'piece'.

# CEANN CROPAIG
### serves 4–6, depending on the size of fish

*On Great Bernera, they advocate adding some chopped onion to the stuffing; and some locals even add a pinch of sugar. My take on it includes kalamata olives as decoration, inserting them into the eye sockets to add a little novelty value; but this is, obviously, by no means traditional!*

1 cod's head, about 2kg (this    1 cod's liver, about 600g
     is the cleaned weight)      (cleaned weight)

Medium oatmeal

First you have to clean the cod's head, which I ask my fishmonger to do for me. Remove the gills, then all the innards come out easily. Leave the lugs on, as these are ideal 'flaps' to close over the stuffing. The eyes should be removed through the back, to give you perfect sockets; if you cut them out from the front, there will be tendons left in. Now wash it all out and dry well.

Now tackle the liver: not a task for the faint-hearted. Cod's liver invariably has lots of tiny worms in it so these should be removed. The simplest way is just to snip away with a sharp knife – or use your fingers. (The worms are creamy white little rings – easy to see.) It is easier than you might think as they are all on the surface, so most come away as you pull at the outer skin. Once all the worms are out, discard any veins, then wash the liver thoroughly and pat dry.

Place in a large bowl with equal quantities of oatmeal – I used 600g for my liver, which was from a large cod. Season well with salt and pepper. The fun begins now as you must get in with your hands and squish everything together until it is thoroughly mixed. The mixture should not be too dry, otherwise the stuffing will become hard. Then stuff the head: I find it easier to position the head in the large pan you are to cook it in, then push in the stuffing, remembering to lift the lugs and tuck in beside the cheeks. You can pack it quite tightly. Close over the flaps to cover – but don't worry if they don't cover completely, the stuffing will not be all enclosed.

Some recipes advise coating the head in flour, to help prevent water seeping into the fish. Pour over about 1.8–2 litres cold water (which will come most of the way up the head) and bring slowly to the boil. Then skim off any scum, cover and cook gently for 30 minutes. (This is the timing for a large cod's head; reduce the time to 20 minutes for a smaller one.) Take off the heat, remove any scum and allow the head to cool in the liquid, still covered, until it is warm, not hot.

Remove the head carefully to an ashet, and if you like, decorate with some greenery such as parsley or watercress; you can also insert a couple of large kalamata olives into the eye sockets to make them look less terrifying. The broth can be kept as a base for a simple fish soup.

When you serve, ensure everyone has a bit of the delicacies – tongue *and* cheek – as well as some stuffing.

# Ceann Cropaig, Harris

A conversation with Hamish Taylor from Flodabay, eastern Harris, is always fascinating. As is often the case with islanders, he is a man of many parts, having been a radio engineer, radio officer in the merchant navy and a fisherman; he loves anything to do with the sea, and boats. He is also the boatman for the island of Pabbay to the south west of Harris, a trip from Leverburgh of some 35 to 40 minutes. The island had a considerable population in past centuries and most of the St Kilda stewards were Pabbay men. In the early nineteenth century the population was estimated at about 100 and they produced corn, barley and illicit whisky! But then it was cleared of its inhabitants in the 1840s to make way for sheep, yet another example of the Highland and island clearances and the valuing of sheep over people by landlords.

The island of Pabbay (the Harris isle, not to be confused with the island of Pabbay south of Barra) is now run as a single sheep farm, and Hamish goes out to take the two or three shepherds there and back. They stay on the otherwise uninhabited island for the duration of the lambing season.

Hamish gave me his recipes using Hebridean lamb and also for one of his favourite dishes, Cormorant Soup (see chapter 2). When I spoke to him back in 1999 for my Scots cooking book, he described to me his version of Ceann Cropaig. He likes to make small fishcakes from the liver, but instead of using cod which is the most common for a Crappit Heid, he prefers to use coley, since there are fewer worms. After washing the fish liver well, he mashes equal quantities of liver with wholemeal flour (again with the hands – their heat helps release fish oil which binds the mixture) and drops little cakes of the mixture into simmering water to poach. Once cooked, they float to the surface and are served with whole boiled fish.

*Harris hills.*

# HAMISH TAYLOR'S CEANN CROPAIG

*serves 4*

*According to Hamish, this was quite a well-known supplement to a staple diet of boiled fish, 'back-in-the-day'. Hamish prefers flour to the standard oatmeal.*

4 medium-sized coarse fish, such as Coley

1 large teaspoon of black pepper

1 large teaspoon of salt

½ a small onion, finely chopped

2 cups of wholemeal plain flour

A good handful of fresh fish livers (washed)

Lay the fish in a large pan and generously cover with salted water and set to boil. While the fish comes to the boil, mix the pepper, salt and onion into the flour.

Gradually add the seasoned flour to the livers, mixing thoroughly with your bare hands. The more you mix, the softer the mixture becomes, so continue adding flour until the mix consistency is so firm that a ball of mixture just begins to slump when laid on a plate. The livers will have been largely transformed into fish-oil by the mixing and the heat of your hands. Form the mixture into small fishcake-shaped patties.

When the water boils, reduce the heat to a simmer and *gently* lay the patties into the water, over the fish. Carefully maintain the heat at a gentle simmer to avoid the patties disintegrating.

Cooking should take about 20 minutes. Generally, when they are cooked, they float. Gently lift them out of the water with a large perforated spoon and lay on a plate. Leave to cool a little, then check by cutting one with a knife. The centre should be fairly dry (the water should not have permeated through it).

Serve with the boiled fish.

# Fish
## (Café Fish, Mull)

Café Fish, a small restaurant on the upper floor of the CalMac booking office on the ferry pier at Tobermory, is owned and run by cousins Jane Gill and Liz McGougan, who were brought up in houses next door to each other on the shores of Loch Fyne in the fishing village of Tarbert. Most of their working lives have been spent in the catering trade, starting off in the early 80s in the family's Anchor Hotel, Tarbert, specialising in fresh Loch Fyne seafood. They opened Café Fish in 2004 and it has since won many awards, including Lonely Planet recommending them as one of their top five restaurants in Scotland and the Good Food Guide rating them as UK Fish Restaurant of the Year in 2012.

The Café is wonderfully appointed, with spectacular views over Tobermory Bay to Calve Island and the Sound of Mull. From the alfresco terrace and from some of the inside tables you can see stunning sunsets to the west. My daughter Jess and I sat looking out over Tobermory Bay as the sun set in a cloudless sky, with plates of garlicky grilled langoustines on the table, each nestling a glass of chilled Muscadet. If you dine earlier, you can also watch the seafood arrive at the restaurant on its own fishing boat, *The Highlander*. Their langoustines, lobster and squat lobster are landed daily at 4 pm, ready for dinner. Other local boats land their monkfish, dover sole, cod, halibut, john dory, haddock, plaice, scallops and squid. Their oysters and crabs come from down the road in Croig, their mussels from nearby Inverlussa. Their smoked salmon is from the Tobermory Fish Company and scallops from Isle of Mull scallops. And they don't only serve fish; their steaks come from the Highland cattle born and bred locally just north at Glengorm Castle.

They serve their fish and shellfish either simply grilled or in a delicate sauce that won't overpower the freshness of the seafood. Their emphasis – on the freshest produce simply cooked – says it all.

# CAFÉ FISH FISH STEW

*Serves 4*

*This is a staple at Café Fish, where it is served sprinkled with gremolata; but chopped parsley is fine too, if you prefer. Serve with plenty of good bread to dunk into the beautifully flavoured garlicky sauce.*

*For the tomato sauce:*

1 onion, peeled and sliced

1 head of fennel, trimmed and sliced

4 cloves of garlic, peeled and finely chopped

1 tbsp dried Italian mixed herbs

1 tsp chilli flakes

60ml olive oil

250ml white wine

3 tins chopped tomatoes

1 bunch basil, chopped

1 level tsp salt

1 level tbsp sugar

*For the fish:*

Approximately 40 mussels, cleaned

150g haddock fillet, chopped

100g smoked haddock fillet, chopped

150g salmon fillet, skinned and chopped

20 queenies (small scallops), cleaned

*For the gremolata:*

1 lemon, zested

6 tbsp olive oil

2 garlic cloves, peeled and crushed

1 small bunch of flatleaf parsley, finely chopped

For the gremolata, mix together the lemon zest, olive oil, garlic and parsley together.

For the tomato sauce and fish, fry the onion, fennel, garlic, mixed herbs and chilli flakes in the olive oil until soft and slightly brown, then add the white wine and boil for

*Looking over the Sound of Mull.*

about 5 minutes. Add the chopped tomatoes (rinsing the tins out with a little water – an extra half to three-quarters of one can or so altogether – and adding this to the mix), bring to the boil and then simmer for about 45 minutes; add the basil, salt and sugar and adjust the seasoning as necessary. Add the mussels, chopped haddock, chopped smoked haddock, chopped salmon and queenies to the tomato sauce and poach lightly until they are cooked, which will take about 8–10 minutes.

Garnish with the gremolata and serve with fresh crusty bread.

# Salt Fish
## (Shetland)

When David Polson worked on the ferries to and from the Shetland island of Whalsay, he used to be given a lot of fish, particularly whiting and haddock. These he would salt in the traditional Shetland way. Using the type of rough sea salt you grit roads with, he would leave it salted for about a week, then would hang it up to dry for a month at least. The salted fish would hang on ropes either above the Raeburn stove or under the gables of the house. It could last years like this, but of course the drier it becomes, the less edible it is; so ideally it would be used after hanging a month or so, when it was ready to reconstitute in water, which also removes the excess salt.

Fast forward several years and David decided to try making salt fish commercially, but the market was not yet ready. When he gave it another go in 2015, however, the demand was great – both from locals who had not forgotten about Shetland's traditional salt fish and also from newer foodies who had come across bacalao, bacalhau or brandade in Spain, Portugal or France.

The traditional Shetland method of salting fish goes back centuries, and one of the most prosperous times for Shetland's salt fish was some 150 years ago when the Basque people traded with these most northerly of Scotland's islands, believing that Shetland's salt cod was the finest in the world.

Now, from his house in the southern mainland of Shetland, David produces the salt cod by removing the head, filleting, skinning and boning the fish before salting for a week. He then dries the fish for some 4–5 weeks before it is ready for packaging under the Thule Ventus label. He also makes it into Brandade de Morue, that salt cod pate so beloved of Provence and Languedoc. For this he uses local Shetland potatoes, cream, buttermilk, garlic and Scottish rapeseed oil. It is good hot or cold, spread on toast or oatcakes.

# SALT COD PÂTÉ

*serves 4*

*For this you can use half cream, half buttermilk to give it a lovely tang; or add a squeeze of lemon at the end instead. Ensure you use as fresh a clove of garlic as possible, not an old stale clove, as that taste will linger.*

*I like to serve it either with wholemeal toast or with Shetland's wonderful Oceanic oatcakes, baked in the most northerly Shetland island, Unst. They are made with oatmeal and sea water.*

*Shetland's Thule Ventus company sells the salt cod in 50g or 250g portions. I like the small pack as it makes a nice bowlful, enough for canapes for many – or lunch for four. If using a larger quantity than in this recipe, then increase the other ingredients accordingly.*

50g salt cod, soaked in cold water according to pack instructions (usually 12–24 hours)

1 medium potato, peeled and cooked

1 fat garlic clove, peeled and crushed

100ml single cream

2–3 tbsp olive oil

Juice of half lemon

Remove the fish from the water and place in a food processor with the potato, garlic and, cream. Process and add the oil through the feeder tube. Then add the lemon juice, black pepper to taste (it should not need salt). The consistency should be a thickish pâté; if too stiff, then add a little more oil. Serve with hot toast or oatcakes.

# OUT SKERRIES STEWED OLICK

*serves 4*

*Before you pass swiftly over this dish, thinking it sounds a little odd, believe me, this is one of the most delicious dishes in the book. Olick is the Shetland dialect for a young ling, and this recipe is based on that of the mother of Martin Johnson, my friend Isabel's husband. Martin's family are all from Out Skerries, to the north east of Shetland. When Martin was growing up there the population was healthy – about 80 – and the economy was thriving. Nowadays, though there is still thankfully a primary school, there are now fewer than 40 inhabitants. Unlike some of the other islands that have a bridge, Out Skerries are too far from mainland Shetland for that, and so to get to Lerwick there is a two and a half hour ferry or a 90-minute ferry to Vidlin, then a 30-minute drive.*

*We discussed many traditional dishes both from Out Skerries and other places in Shetland including Proag, Stap and Krappin. Proag is a Skerries dish of fish livers melted in a pan and poured over boiled flaked fish and potatoes. Stap, which is known all over Shetland, involves roasting fish livers, usually olick (ling) or piltock (young saithe or coalfish) and mixing together with boiled flaked fish. Krappin is Shetland's version of Crappit Heid – fish livers mixed with oatmeal, stuffed into the fish head, then boiled, or steamed in greaseproof paper or foil parcels.*

*This stewed olick dish was made by Mary Johnson regularly for her family on Out Skerries. There are basically two ingredients – fish and onions – but it is incomparably good.*

4 thick, middle-cut fillets of ling, skinned

1–2 tbsp seasoned flour

Mild olive oil (Mary would have used white fat, possibly lard, or butter)

2 large onions, peeled and sliced into rings

*Out Skerries Stewed Olick*

Dip the fish in the flour. Heat the oil over a medium high heat and add the fish. Cook for a minute or so until browned on one side, then turn and add the onions. Cook for another couple of minutes or so until the onions begin to brown.

Add about a half cup of water, enough just to prevent burning, and reduce the heat to low. Continue to cook for about 15 minutes until most of the water has evaporated and the fish is just cooked and the onions brown. Serve on warm plates with tatties and a green vegetable.

# Halibut
# (Gigha)

The Gigha Boathouse opens for seven months of the year only; but during that time, Chef Gordon MacNeil and his team are rushed off their feet. For a restaurant that can seat 36 people, it is not unusual in midsummer for them to serve up to 100 lunches, and up to 60 dinners. Since it is only 20 minutes on the ferry over from Tayinloan to Gigha, there are many who come over from the mainland just for lunch.

Chef Gordon MacNeil was born on Gigha, at Kinrerach Farm in the north, but brought up in Glasgow. Having worked as a chef in Glasgow, then at Gleneagles under legendary pastry chef Ian Ironside, he moved south. After many years away, he returned to the island of his birth where the owner of the Boathouse was looking for a chef. This was back in 2013, when it was more a café serving good food; but gradually Gordon and his team have built it up into an award-winning restaurant, where seafood is a speciality. Obviously halibut stars on the menu, since Gigha halibut has been sustainably farmed in the seas off the island since 2006. Here is one of the most popular Gigha Boathouse dishes using the local halibut.

# GIGHA HALIBUT WITH SHELLFISH BROTH
*serves 4*

*I have adapted this recipe from Gordon's; he serves it with a wonderful Jerusalem artichoke and truffle mash, easily made by cooking the artichokes in milk, then pureeing with butter and adding truffle oil to taste.*

4 x 250g fillets of halibut, skinned

Olive oil

Juice of 1 lemon

Knob of butter

1 litre fish stock

6 cloves garlic

½ a red chilli, cleaned and chopped

2 lime leaves

1 stalk of lemongrass

1 red pepper, cleaned, and sliced

1 red onion, peeled, and sliced

Knob of fresh ginger, peeled and grated

1 tsp of brown sugar

*To finish:*

A good handful each of langoustine tails (peeled), mussels (scrubbed) and cockles (cleaned)

1 red pepper, cleaned and thinly sliced

1 carrot, peeled and thinly sliced

A handful of fresh coriander, chopped

Rub the halibut in the olive oil, salt, pepper and lemon juice. Heat a large frying pan to very hot and add the fish. Sear till brown all over and place in a hot oven (220C/425F/Gas 7) for 2 minutes, then remove and add the butter. Keep somewhere warm for ten minutes or so.

Heat the stock, add the next 8 ingredients and salt and pepper. Bring to the boil, simmer for 5 minutes or so, then strain, removing and discarding the lime leaves and lemongrass. Puree the remaining bits in the sieve with some of the stock before returning this puree to the stock. Taste for seasoning, then return to the heat and bring the stock to a rolling boil. Add the langoustines, mussels and cockles, cook for a minute or so just until the mussels and cockles open, then remove from the heat.

To serve, ladle the broth into four warm bowls, top with coriander and place the halibut in the middle. If serving with artichoke puree, top with a spoonful (or cheffy quenelle!) of that. Eat with a spoon and fork.

*Sun setting in the Hebrides.*

*Opposite: Scallops, Sconsor, Skye.*

# 4
# Shellfish

# Crab
## (Islay)

Jim McFarlane has lived in Port Ellen on the southern tip of the island of Islay since he was born seven decades ago. Having fished since he was 12, he knows a thing or two about the art. And so as he explained to me how it has changed over the years, he also showed me his hand-built wooden 'sgoth' (Gaelic for skiff), which was the traditional Islay fishing boat for some 200 years, from the mid-eighteenth century.

But first, the changes in Islay fishing: when Jim started it was primarily for lobsters, with crab being more of a by-product. The lobsters were all sent to London, by ferry and rail, in tea-chests packed with bracken and heather. Nowadays, with lobster stocks depleted, it is crab the Islay fishermen bring in, mainly large brown crabs but also velvet crabs to which the Spaniards are partial. Since the early 1980s the vivier trucks have transported Islay shellfish to Spain. Jim tells me how he also 'scalloped' for 20 years, the treasured shellfish going direct to the Continent. After the 'golden years', as Jim calls it, from 1975 to 1985, fishing changed on Islay as everywhere else. Now stocks are depleted, most is sent off to Spain and France and there are fewer local young men who want to become fishermen any more. For the past few years, Jim has been fishing for mackerel, not to sell, but for the 'creel boys' to use as bait to lure the lobsters and crabs into their creels. Fortunately, however, there are more local restaurants now using Islay shellfish, such as crab claws, freshly boiled lobster and seafood platters.

Sadly, nowadays, no-one on Islay continues the centuries-old island tradition of air-drying or salt-curing saithe or lythe; or hanging up skate wings for a week before skinning, then boiling them and eating on a daily basis. But now that tourists can order the wonderful Islay crab, lobster and scallops in restaurants and locals can buy them, all is not lost. And certainly things have improved from two or three decades ago when all the seafood catch was sent off to France or Spain. At last, we Scots are also appreciating the wonderful produce around our shores and hanging onto at least some of it.

# CRAB SANDWICH

*serves 1*

*Here is Jim McFarlane's famous crab sandwich. To cook his crab, Jim recommends placing in cold water, then slowly bringing it to the boil. This prevents the claws from being cast, which happens if they are plunged directly, as you do for lobsters, into boiling water.*

2 slices of brown bread, buttered

About 90g crabmeat (half white, half brown or – Jim's preference – all brown)

1 thin slice of smoked salmon

Freshly squeezed lemon juice

Horseradish sauce, optional

Spread one slice of bread with the brown meat, then white meat if using, and lay the salmon on top. Give a good squeeze of lemon all over, then, if using, smear a little horseradish on the other slice of bread before clamping this onto on the lower slice, cutting and devouring. Hungrily.

*Port Ellen, Islay.*

# ISLAY WHISKY RAREBIT ON WHOLEMEAL SODA BREAD

*Rarebit serves 2–3; soda bread makes 2 loaves*

*Emma and Ron Goudie opened their wonderful B&B, The Old Excise House, on Islay in 2010, since when it has had nothing but glowing reviews. Formerly the Excise House for Laphroaig Distillery, it is now a luxury bed and breakfast, close to the village of Port Ellen and within walking distance of the whisky distilleries of Ardbeg, Lagavulin and Laphroaig. It is a glorious place to unwind.*

*Emma is an excellent cook, baking different items for the guests' breakfasts every day. Her soda bread is a favourite and she also uses it for cheese on toast or to accompany seafood platters, or in another delicious dish she makes, Crab Rarebit, using local Islay crab from Ishbel and Frazer at the Islay Seafood Shack.*

## WHOLEMEAL SODA BREAD

*makes 2 small loaves*

| | |
|---|---|
| 225g wholemeal flour | 1 medium free-range egg |
| 225g plain flour | 350ml buttermilk |
| 1 tsp bicarbonate of soda | 50g coarse oatmeal (Emma uses Golspie Mill) |
| 3 tsp baking powder | |
| 1 tsp salt | |

Place the wholemeal flour in a bowl, and sieve onto it the plain flour, bicarbonate of soda, baking powder and salt. Mix together and make a well in the centre.

Beat the egg and buttermilk together, pour into the well and stir with wooden spoon, until it is a fairly soft dough (add extra buttermilk if needed). Quickly turn onto a floured surface, flour your hands and form an even round shape, cut into two and shape each half gently into an oval around 4cm deep.

Transfer onto a lightly greased baking tray with space between each loaf and sprinkle the tops with coarse oatmeal. Bake in a preheated oven (190C/375F/Gas 5) for 40 minutes. Remove from the oven and cool on a cooling rack for at least 30 minutes before cutting.

# ISLAY WHISKY CRAB RAREBIT
*serves 3–4*

*Ron Goudie prefers to call the Rarebit a Harebit, as he says there are far more hares than rabbits on Islay!*
*Even though there only is a tiny amount of Islay whisky in this dish, the smoky peat flavour sings through the fabulous concoction.*

125g mature Cheddar-style cheese (Emma likes Mull of Kintyre or Isle of Mull)

3 medium (or 2 large) free-range egg yolks

1 tbsp Worcestershire sauce

1 tsp Dijon mustard

6 drops tabasco

30ml Ardbeg 10-year-old malt whisky

175g white crab meat plus 50g brown crab meat (or 225g white if preferred)

6–8 slices (cut medium, not thick) of the soda bread or sourdough loaf

Roasted cherry tomatoes and rocket, to serve

Mix all the ingredients together in a bowl, apart from the bread and crab. Season to taste with the salt and pepper. Just before grilling fold the crab meat in through the mixture.

Toast the bread on one side under the grill. Spread the cheesy crab mixture evenly on top and grill until browned and puffed up. Eat on its own or garnished with roasted cherry tomatoes and rocket.

# Crab
## (Skye)

Donnie MacDonald's family have been crofters on the south-west of Skye overlooking Tarskavaig Bay, between Achnacloich and Tarskavaig, since the early nineteenth century when the villages were created. Donnie's father, one of twelve children, left the villages to find work, but his family would return each Easter and for extended summer breaks. That is how Donnie learned all about fishing and crofting – and now he continues to appreciate the glorious views his ancestors enjoyed for decades from his house on the croft land overlooking the bay and across to Rum and Canna. On a clear day he can see as far as Barra and South Uist.

He and his family love to go out in his fishing boat to catch mainly pollack and coalfish – mackerel in the summer months, cod in winter. Shellfish (mussels and razor clams) are abundant on the coast and are a source of an occasional treat. But it is lobster and crabs from his lobster pots that his daughters particularly love to feast on, although he tells me that these were never cooked at home in his parents' day. Historically few shellfish were eaten by locals as, during the Clearances, the people were pushed off their fertile land onto the coast where they were forced to survive on shellfish. The memories of this as a 'poor man's' food – with its shameful connotations – lingered well into the late twentieth century. Nowadays thankfully crab and lobster are eaten once more with great pleasure.

*Donnie MacDonald.*

# CRAB 'RISOTTO' WITH QUINOA

*serves 2 as main course; 3–4 as starter*

*This is Donnie's wife Bea's recipe for crab risotto: not a risotto in the true sense as the main element in a risotto – rice – is not present. Bea makes this delicious dish with quinoa, a protein-rich grain grown high on the Andes that has become more and more popular over the years. It is lighter than a rich butter-laden risotto and makes a welcome change.*

*To cook the crab, boil freshly caught crab for 15–20 minutes at a rolling boil then, once it has cooled, extract the white meat from the pincers. The brown meat can also be used for this dish but white meat is preferable.*

| | |
|---|---|
| 500ml vegetable stock | 1 large cup (250ml) of frozen peas, defrosted slightly |
| 25g butter | 200g cooked white crab meat |
| 1 small onion, peeled and finely chopped | Zest of 1 lemon, grated |
| 1–2 cloves garlic, peeled and finely chopped | A small handful of herbs (parsley/chives/dill), chopped |
| 200g quinoa | |
| 250ml dry white wine | |

First heat the stock in a pan and keep fairly hot. In a separate pan, melt the butter and cook the onion and garlic gently until softened, then add the quinoa and cook until the grains begin to stick slightly to the pan.

Add the wine, stir well and allow the mixture to bubble for a minute or two, then add the hot stock, a ladle at a time, allowing the liquid to be absorbed before adding more – just as you would with a regular risotto. If you need more liquid, add hot water to the stock pan.

Test the quinoa and when it still has a good bite to it, add the peas and continue cooking. When quinoa and peas are cooked, add the crab and heat through gently. Season to taste with lemon zest, a little salt and plenty of ground black pepper. Garnish with chopped herbs and serve in warm bowls.

# Oysters
## (Islay and Skye)

Craig Archibald and his father Tony began farming oysters as a sideline to their cattle, sheep, barley and oats, on the shores of Loch Gruinart on the north of Islay in 1988. The spats, aged about 3–6 months, arrive on the island and grow until they are about two years old. They have been described in print and verbally all over the island as 'the greatest oysters in the Northern hemisphere'; they are indeed almost uniquely plump and juicy. The reason for this is because the two must-haves for oyster cultivation are an abundant supply of clear water and plankton, the oysters' staple diet. Loch Gruinart has both. The Archibalds farm the Pacific oyster which can be eaten all year round, unlike the native European oysters which breed during the summer months. And it is not only the year-round availability that makes them so sought after, it is their year-round consistent quality.

Because they have the Gulf Stream to warm the water in winter and the usual Scottish weather means temperatures never rise too much, the water remains more or less the same temperature, which is ideal for oysters. Because Loch Gruinart is an estuary, it is tidal and so the oysters spend their lives filtering the nutrient-rich sea water, which is changed twice a day by the tide. Like all oysters, they are low in fat and high in vitamins and minerals, zinc in particular.

Just like the excellent Islay lamb, beef, pork and like other shellfish, more and more Islay oysters are being sold locally, to Islay chefs who cook them or, more often, serve them raw with nothing more than a glass of chilled white wine. Nowadays an astonishing 30,000 of the Archibalds' oysters are sold each year on Islay, which is not bad going for a population of some 3,000. As well as the restaurants ordering them in, the locals can buy them direct from their farm these days. Craig told me their oysters are officially the best in Scotland, as judged from 2015-16 to 2016-17 at the Association of Scottish Shellfish Growers conference. An accolade indeed, considering how many oyster farmers there are now across the islands and mainland.

In one of the Islay hotels, you might be offered a local Finlaggan Ale with a plate of oysters. The other obvious choice is of course whisky, given the eight world-famous distilleries on this small Hebridean island. Many people (but never locals: that would be sacrilege) drizzle their Islay oysters with some malt, the best match being the less peaty ones such as Bunnahabhain or Bruichladdich. Tony likes to toss freshly opened oysters into an omelette or remove the top shell and grill with a splash of cream and some grated cheese.

*Skye oysters.*

Craig told me that it is 'rubbish' that some so-called oyster experts insist you must only swallow, never chew oysters. Certainly for first-timers, chewing makes the oysters less of a challenge.

The appreciation of oysters has spread across the islands over the years. On the western coast of Skye, just beyond the Talisker distillery in Calbost, is The Oyster Shed. Kenny Bain established an oyster farm on Loch Harport in 1981 and steadily expanded the business over the years. When his son-in-law, Paul McGlynn, took over the business in 2008, the capacity of oyster production had increased so much they decided to open a farm shop to sell them. Soon they also offered local seafood platters and takeaway food such as Loch Harport crab and prawn (langoustine) rolls and homemade fish soup.

I found it interesting to see Japanese, German and American tourists walk up the steep hill behind the distillery swinging their Talisker bags with bottles just bought in the distillery shop. They were heading up to The Oyster Shed for lunch outdoors overlooking the loch. It could have been Spain or the south of France, with that wonderful seafood and a fabulous view over the water, but it was Skye and there was whisky and that was a joy to see.

*To open an oyster*: Wrap your left hand in a tea towel. Place an oyster – cup-side down, hinge towards you – in the palm. Insert an oyster knife into the hinge, push and twist simultaneously, passing the knife under the top shell to cut the muscle, sliding along the length to fully open. Retain all juices.

# OYSTERS WITH SAUSAGES
*serves 4*

*The combination of hot and cold here is divine!*

500g sausages, halved (beef or pork, with a high meat content)

16–20 oysters

Grill the sausages, place on a dish. Open the oysters, place on ice alongside. Eat a hot sausage, then a cold oyster.

# BEEF AND OYSTER PIE
*serves 4*

*Serve with mashed potatoes and stir-fried kail or savoy cabbage.*

750 g rump steak, very thinly sliced

8 oysters

1 heaped tbsp seasoned flour

50g butter

2 onions, peeled and chopped

250ml beef stock, boiling

375g packet of ready-rolled puff pastry

Beaten egg

Cut the steak slices in two and lay on a board. Open the oysters, remove from the shell and retain the juices. Wrap each oyster in a piece of beef and dip in flour. Place snugly in a 1.5 litre oven dish. Season. Melt the butter in a saucepan, fry the onions until tender and tip over the beef. Pour over the oyster juices and boiling stock. Cover tightly, cook at 160C/325F/Gas 3 for 1½ hours. Remove and cool.

Moisten the edges of the dish and place the pastry on top. Trim, pressing to seal, brush with egg, and slit the top twice. Bake at 220C/425F/Gas 7 for about 25 minutes until golden brown.

## Scallops
### (Skye)

Diving for scallops is not easy. On the day I visited Sconser and met father and son David and Ben Oakes as they dragged their boat up onto the shore just before the Raasay ferry came in, the effects of Hurricane Ophelia were still being felt all over Scotland. The churning water was grey and forbidding, and yet the two men had no choice but to put on their diving gear and venture out into the middle of Loch Sligachan. They had customers to please. David said it was difficult to see anything down there, and they had to find the perfect size of scallops by feel from the seabed. Working three to four days a week to fulfil orders from restaurants all over Skye, including The Three Chimneys, Loch Bay and Stein Inn, they also have online orders.

Scallop-diving has always been a difficult way of making a living and yet, when David left his job in civil engineering diving some three decades ago, he was drawn to the coast of Skye and to this sea loch where he started his scallop venture in 1988. His initial technique was to catch and cultivate from spat (the juvenile bivalves) then re-lay in what is known as the several order (the piece of seabed where only Sconser Scallops are allowed to harvest) when the scallops had reached over 50mm and were about two years old. Nowadays, however, there is natural regeneration for stocking these sustainably grown shellfish.

On the grey blustery day I visited, David pointed out to me where his several order lies, in the second fifth of the sea loch. It is the perfect stretch of water for this, as the first fifth, the water at the loch head in front of Hotel Sligachan, near the Red and Black Cuillin, is too tidal. The next fifth is too brackish, the next too wild and so theirs, the second fifth from the sea, is perfect on all counts.

*David and Ben, scallop fishermen.*

As I watched David and Ben lug the nets full of beautiful scallops up to their van on the slipway, I thought nothing looked perfect to me, apart from those beautiful scallops. This was hard work, only undertaken by dedicated divers. And it didn't end there: they would grab a quick bite of lunch, then drive all over Skye to deliver their catch to the restaurants so that diners could taste them that evening at dinner. That's service for you.

# DAVID OAKES' SCALLOP TEMPURA WITH DIPPING SAUCE

*serves 4*

*David says these are so delicious, the family usually eat them before they're all cooked, while he is still standing at the cooker. David no longer eats gluten and so uses gluten-free flour, but a mixture of regular wheat flour and rice flour will also do in his recipe.*

*I have left the measurements in cups as that is how David cooks. He uses a small mug or regular teacup with a capacity of 150ml of liquid.*

*Chilli dipping sauce:*

1 red chilli, de-seeded and chopped extremely fine

½ cup red wine vinegar

1 heaped tbsp of caster sugar

*Scallops and batter:*

16 scallops, roe removed

1 cup of gluten-free plain flour, seasoned

Sparkling mineral water or tonic water

Good quality sunflower oil (preferably cold-pressed) for deep frying in a wok

Lemon slices to serve

For the sauce, warm the vinegar and sugar gently in a small pan till the sugar dissolves, then add the chilli. Leave up to a couple of hours for the flavours to develop.

Slice the scallops in half horizontally and leave sitting on kitchen roll to dry out while preparing the batter.

For the batter, put the flour in a bowl and gradually mix in enough of the sparkling/tonic water to make a batter similar in consistency to a watery single cream.

Heat about 5cm of the sunflower oil in a wok to smoking point, dip 4 scallop halves at a time into the batter, place into the wok and cook till they are golden and come free easily from the bottom; then turn them over and cook for another minute or so. Remove using a slotted spoon or tongs (allow the oil to drip back into the wok) and put onto a heatproof dish lined with kitchen roll to catch more of the oil, and keep warm till all the scallops are cooked.

Serve with the dipping sauce and lemon slices.

# Seafood
## (Scalpay)

When the bridge from Harris to the Outer Hebridean isle of Scalpay, a mere 300 metres away, was opened in 1997, there must have been celebrations throughout the small island; it is only some two and a half miles long but with a healthy population of nearly 300. One feature that has encouraged even more people since then to cross over the bridge to Scalpay is the North Harbour Bistro. Opened in 2014 by Chef George Lavery, it has already gained many awards, including the prestigious 'Islands Restaurant of the Year' in 2017. George trained at Anniesland College, then worked in various establishments, including in Jersey where he trained under eminent chef David Cameron, and for a couple of years in Ireland. Later he was one of a team of top chefs who would cook at Wimbledon, Ascot and Lords for the season and then work in the French Alps in the winter.

After a walk the length of the small island to the lighthouse and back, I sat in the Scalpay bistro looking out onto the water just outside and to the jetty where all George's shellfish is landed. Taking in the tranquillity and the Hebridean beauty and wildness, I had to ask what brought him here, to one of the most remote places in the country, such a change from the glitz of Royal Ascot. He told me he had been home in Glasgow and had seen something in the paper about the Isle of Harris, then he saw an old film mentioning Harris Tweed. So he phoned a hotel in Tarbert in Harris, and was asked to send his CV. The rest is history: after some four years working on Harris, he had a call from the Scalpay Development Community Trust asking if he was interested in running the bistro. He was so successful at this, he was eventually asked if he would like to buy it outright, which of course he did. In the summer months, it is so busy, he has to turn guests away from his 30-seater restaurant; and for such high-end cooking that would not be out of place in Edinburgh or London, this is perhaps surprising. But when you consider that on his doorstep is some of the best seafood, meat and game in the UK, it makes sense.

It is not unusual for George and his small team of chefs to cook for 50 at lunch and then 70 in two sittings at dinner, and inevitably they had to turn away people wanting just a cup of tea and a slice of cake. So when the opportunity came to buy the shop adjacent to the bistro, George did so, and now that is running as a café selling simple lunches and cakes baked by a local Scalpay lady. In the bistro kitchen, George uses local eggs from Anna just along the road, meat from a Stornoway butcher, fish from the Hebridean waters and of course the shellfish landed right outside the kitchen window. On the two nights I dined there, I tried various dishes, including Sole 'Toast' with Scallop, Seafood Chowder

*Scalpay.*

and Scallop and Crab Ravioli, but the following two recipes were among my favourites. The black pudding, 'prawn' and chorizo starter uses langoustines (prawn is the local word for langoustine) landed two minutes from the kitchen on the new Scalpay pier. And the crab soufflé was a revelation, so light and delicate.

# CRAB SOUFFLÉ

*serves 6*

*George serves this with a delicate salad at the Scalpay bistro.*

| | |
|---|---|
| 50g butter | 5 free-range egg whites |
| 50g self-raising flour | A handful of chopped chives |
| 150 ml hot milk | 200g crabmeat |
| 2 free-range egg yolks | |
| 100g mild goats cheese, crumbled or chopped | |

Butter 6 ramekins really well and refrigerate.

Melt butter, add flour, make a roux and add hot milk gradually, whisking to keep it smooth. Add egg yolks and cheese and season with salt and pepper.

Whisk the egg whites until stiff and add the chives. Add the crab to the cheese mixture, gently fold in half of the egg whites, then fold in the rest.

Fill ramekins to the top, level with a palette knife and run your finger around the rim to ensure even rising; then sit the ramekins in a deep oven tray of boiling water and bake at 180C/350F/Gas 4 for 20 to 25 minutes.

# SCALPAY LANGOUSTINE WITH BLACK PUDDING, CHORIZO AND PEA PURÉE

*serves 2*

*George uses black pudding from Ness on the northern tip of Lewis. He makes his pea puree by sautéing the shallots in a little butter, adding 400g cooked petit pois peas and some salt, then blending to a purée with 60ml milk.*

| | |
|---|---|
| 4 small slices of black pudding (or 2 regular, cut in quarters), skin removed | 4 plump langoustines |
| | Pea purée |
| Olive oil | Delicate salad leaves |
| 4 small slices of chorizo, skin removed | |

Cook the black pudding in a frying pan with a tiny smear of olive oil until done, then remove and keep warm. Add the chorizo to the pan and cook until done, then remove, keep warm and retain the now orange-coloured oil in the pan.

Meanwhile, cook the langoustines in boiling water for 3–4 minutes, then plunge into cold water and remove the shells. Add the langoustines to the pan, tossing them to coat in the oil.

Arrange the black pudding, chorizo and langoustines artistically on a plate, dollop small spoons of the pea purée all around and drizzle over the chorizo oil.

Islay House Hotel, which dates from the early 1600s, is the impressive building sitting at the head of Lochindaal, with sweeping views across the water of the Kilchoman Peninsula. The chef who set up the kitchen and restaurant was Alex Floyd, who came to fame at Michelin-starred Leith's restaurant in London, where he was Chef Director for ten years. In 2002, he moved to Brazil where he ran a successful restaurant, but then was lured back home to Scotland by an offer to head up Islay House kitchens in 2018.

According to him, the best food on the Scottish islands is simple fare (though elegantly so), with an emphasis on local ingredients. The lamb, beef and venison are all sourced from Islay, as is the shellfish. And halibut from nearby Gigha is always a popular dish on the menu. At Islay House there is a well-established kitchen garden for vegetables, fruits and herbs. Here is Alex's recipe for scallops with black pudding farofa, the latter influenced by his years in Brazil.

# SEARED SCALLOPS WITH BLACK PUDDING FAROFA AND POTATO PURÉE

*serves 4*

*Farofa is a wonderful Brazilian dish that is usually served with the fabulous pork and bean casserole, Feijoada. I loved eating farofa on my visits to Rio or Sao Paulo as, strangely, it reminded me in texture of skirlie. Instead of being made from oatmeal and fried in dripping, however, farofa is made from cassava flour and fried in dende (palm oil) until nutty and toasty.*

*Alex has taken this concept and brilliantly converted it into a Scottish dish by combining Stornoway black pudding with panko crumbs to make a delicious toasty black pudding crumble to serve with scallops. He pairs it with a watercress and potato velouté, which although delicious is rather cheffy, so instead I like to serve with a watercress salad.*

| | |
|---|---|
| 12 large scallops, shelled and cleaned, roes removed | 120g panko bread crumbs |
| | *Potato puree:* |
| 3-4 tbsp rapeseed oil for frying | 4 medium-sized floury potatoes, peeled and diced |
| A squeeze of lemon juice | |
| *Black pudding farofa:* | 4 tbsp double cream |
| 200g Stornoway black pudding, sliced, skin removed | 4 tbsp milk |
| | 60g butter |

Start by preparing the farofa. Place the black pudding on a baking sheet and place in a pre-heated oven at 120C/250F/Gas ½ for about an hour and 15 minutes, then add the breadcrumbs and cook for a further 30 minutes, remove and blend in a mixer until fine.

Place the diced potatoes into a pan, cover with cold water and add a pinch of salt; cover with a lid, bring to the boil, reduce the heat and cook until tender. Drain the potatoes and return to a low heat to dry them well for a couple of minutes, then mash with a masher, mix in the cream, milk and butter while still hot, season to taste and set aside.

Cut the scallops in half if very large and thick; if not leave them whole. Season with salt and pepper. Heat a good heavy-based, non-stick pan with the oil and sear the scallops on both sides – if cut in half, place the cut side into the base of the pan first. Cook for a couple of minutes or so on either side (less if halved) until just cooked, then finish with a little squeeze of lemon juice.

To finish, put a spoonful of the warm potato purée on each plate, divide the just seared scallops between the plates placing over the purée, sprinkle with the black pudding farofa and garnish with some watercress.

# Lobsters
## (Great Bernera)

On the island of Great Bernera, off the west coast of Lewis, there is a famous lobster pond. This is a holding pond where lobsters were kept until they grew to a good size and were more valuable.

Although there are many lobster ponds throughout Lewis and Harris, the Bernera pond is unique for its size and for its history. We do not know who first built such a pond or where the idea came from, but this is one of the first to be constructed. The man who built it was Murdo Morrison, a fisherman, who was born in Croir around 1827. Murdo was a man of vision who achieved much. He planned the dam for the pond and marked the two ends with large stones, then went off to Australia to earn the money required to build it.

There are many tales of his time in Australia, but one astonishing fact is that he worked his passage out there and within two years he had enough money to pay for his passage home and to build his dam, a stone dyke some 75 yards long across the mouth of a narrow inlet, to form a pond some 400 yards long.

The construction of the dam in the 1860s with its curved and tapering shape is a feat of engineering, especially for an untrained man. The workforce was local men and it is said that many women worked there also, carrying the smaller stones in creels on their backs.

Before there were ponds, the fishermen sent their lobsters live to Billingsgate, a journey by cart, bus, boats and trains, and as the prime season for catching lobsters is July and August, the hottest time of the year, this meant that many died on the way. Often fishermen got a telegram from their agents in London saying 'All dead on arrival'. Murdo would therefore buy the fishermen's catch and keep it in the pond until conditions improved. Creels would be set in the pond to recapture the lobsters, which would then be sent south and fetch better prices.

The pond was in use more or less continuously by his descendants and later by the Crofters Supply Agency until the 1960s, since when air freight out of Stornoway has been used.

Here is a lovely recipe in *The Modern Crofters Cookbook* from the Great Bernera Museum for a simple lobster paté.

# LOBSTER PATÉ

*serves 4*

2 tbsp mayonnaise

3 tbsp cream cheese

100g butter, softened

250g (approx.) lobster meat, chopped

cayenne pepper

Mix the first three ingredients in a food processor, then add lobster, a dash of cayenne, salt and pepper, and process briefly.

Chill before serving with oatcakes or toast.

# DONALD MACLENNAN'S LOBSTER 'THERMIDOR'

*serves 2*

*This is Lewis fisherman Donald MacLennan's easy lobster recipe. He generally fishes in more offshore grounds, with less chance of damage to the lobster pots in bad weather; there is a mixed fishery of brown crab and lobster where he goes, from the west of Uig on Lewis to the west of the Monach Islands. He reckons the average size of lobster where he fishes is larger, because of the nature of the seabed: it is different to the shallow Hebridean shoreline which is very rocky and battered by thousands of years' worth of stormy seas. Here there are lots of small nooks and crannies, therefore lots of surface area for smaller lobsters to live amongst. Further offshore grounds, however, are deeper, and although still rocky, the seabed is not broken down as much. Bigger nooks and crannies mean bigger lobsters, in his opinion, but he stresses he could very well be wrong in his lobster-sizing theory!*

*Though he now works out of Leverburgh on Harris, he is a Lewis man, born and bred. He loves to cook a thermidor which he makes without the shells, unlike the classic dish that uses the shells to hold the lobster meat mixed with the other ingredients. Since he gets such a good price for his catch, he seldom eats lobsters himself, but if he catches any with no claws, due to fighting, then these are the ones he takes home for a dinner time treat. He and his wife Catriona like to eat this dish with home-made chips and a glass of chilled white wine.*

| | |
|---|---|
| 25g butter | A handful of parsley, chopped |
| 2–3 fat shallots, peeled and chopped | The cooked flesh of 1 average-size lobster, chopped |
| ½ glass of dry white wine | |
| 250–300ml fish stock | A handful of grated cheese (Donald likes manchego; parmesan is also good) |
| 100ml double cream | |
| 1 tsp English mustard | A handful of fresh breadcrumbs |
| The juice of 1 lemon | |

Melt the butter in a pan, sauté the shallots till softened and add the wine, then the stock and the cream. Add the lemon juice, salt and plenty of freshly ground black pepper and let it bubble away until it reduces down a little. Stir in the parsley and then tip half of the mixture over each of the portions of lobster, which should be in two small ovenproof dishes. Mix then top with the cheese and breadcrumbs – clamping this down with the palms of your hands.

Pop under a hot grill until everything is piping hot and the cheesy topping golden. Serve with home-made chips.

# LANGOUSTINES SERVED WITH GARLIC AND PARSLEY BUTTER
*serves 2*

*My daughter Jess and I had this exquisite dish at Café Fish, Tobermory, Mull, one sun-kissed Sunday evening at the end of April. We had climbed some of Ben More before the rain stopped us halfway up, so we drove up to Calgary beach on the north west of the island and could not believe our eyes. The rain had completely cleared and the scene was more Caribbean than Hebridean, with the clean white sand and sea glistening under an unusually hot sun. There was not a cloud in the sky, and though there was a scattering of people around, it still felt tranquil and idyllic, Scotland at its best.*

12 whole langoustines

100g salted butter

5 cloves of garlic, peeled and finely chopped

2 tbsp fresh flat-leaf parsley, finely chopped

1 tbsp fresh chives, finely chopped

Fresh rustic bread

Lemon wedges

Bring a pan of water to a rolling boil (about 3 litres/5 pints of water for 12 langoustines). Without overcrowding the pan, add the langoustines and cook for 3 to 4 minutes, taking care not to overcook them. You can tell if they're ready by checking the underside of the

*Langoustines, Mull.*

tail: when cooked the flesh will have turned white as opposed to translucent. Remove from the pan and drain.

Meanwhile, soften the butter and add the garlic, flat-leaf parsley (reserving a small amount for serving) and chives to the butter.

Split the langoustines in half and place on a grill pan, dot the butter over the langoustines and place under a hot grill until the butter has melted and langoustines have browned slightly, which will take a minute or so depending on the heat of your grill.

To serve, place the langoustines in a serving dish and pour the (by now melted) garlic butter over. Serve with fresh rustic bread and lemon wedges and sprinkle with remaining parsley.

## Tiree Lobster and Crab

Tiree-born and bred Frazer MacInnes used to fish for lobster and crab with his grandfather from 8 years old. Then, from the age of 14, he got his own boat with his own creels that he puts out a couple of miles along the southern shore of the island. Now, aged 32, he juggles the fishing among other jobs, as so often happens on the islands. Frazer and his partner Ruth Mackinnon, another Tiree local, run a catering trailer in Scarinish, Tiree Lobster and Crab, selling wonderful seafood and drinks. They are open from May through to October, to tie in with the season when the creels are out. They supply fresh lobster and crab from his own boat (they are kept in cages in the harbour alongside the trailer and hauled up when someone wants to buy live lobster or crab) and also a wide range of other fresh seafood, such as scallops, from other boats on Tiree. The fresh seafood is sold to tourists and also to local hotels. He also sells langoustines and prawns from Oban, as well as Tiree beef, lamb and pork direct from the family farm in Ruaig on the north east of the island.

Ruth runs the trailer on her own while Frazer is out on his boat and she sells teas, coffees, soups, cold drinks and ice cream as well as the fresh seafood and Ruaig meat. In order to learn how to make dressed crab, she watched a chef demonstrate it on YouTube. The first one she attempted herself took her 45 minutes; now she can dress 10 crabs in 45 minutes!

The Tiree Lobster and Crab trailer's bestsellers are lobster rolls and Ruaig steak baguettes, both ridiculously easy to make, but both depending on top quality ingredients, preferably from Tiree.

# TIREE LOBSTER BAGUETTE

*serves 1*

*Ruth at the Tiree Lobster and Crab trailer cooks her lobsters by bringing a large pan of water to the boil then dropping in the lobster. Once the water has returned to the boil, she cooks it for about 5 minutes before she removes it and allows to cool – it continues to cook as it cools, so she thinks 5 minutes is fine for a medium-sized lobster – 500-600g. (I prefer to pop the lobster first in the freezer for an hour, then I cook it for a little longer: 15 minutes per 450g, then an extra 10 minutes for every 450g thereafter.) Once it is cool, Ruth says to lay it on its back, cut down the middle and remove and discard the 'gunky bits'! Then take the flesh from the tail and claws.*

*Ruth says she used to offer brown wholemeal baguettes, but customers were only interested in the white bread.*

| | |
|---|---|
| The cooked flesh from half a medium (or one small) lobster | Tabasco |
| 2 tbsp mayonnaise | Lemon juice |
| 2 tbsp tomato ketchup | 1 x 30cm baguette, buttered |

Mix the lobster with the mayonnaise and ketchup, add a dash of tabasco and squirt of lemon juice then pile into the buttered baguette. Devour at once. Messily.

# SCALLOWAY HOTEL LOBSTER WITH GARLIC BUTTER AND POTATO SALAD

*serves 2*

*Whenever I visit Shetland, the one place I always like to visit is the Scalloway Hotel. Not only is the view wonderful – on the waterfront in Scalloway, Shetland's former capital – but the food superb. Peter and Caroline MacKenzie have run the hotel for the past twelve years and pride themselves on using local produce – Shetland lamb and beef, white fish, excellent salad leaves and vegetables from Turriefield on the west coast near Sandness; and of course the wonderful shellfish come from the waters all around. They get their crab and lobsters from Jim Black who fishes off the south of mainland Shetland, between Fair Isle and Shetland. On my last visit, I had the lobster and it was one of the most simple – yet finest – lobster dishes I have eaten. Always messy, but so delicious.*

*Here is the recipe of Scalloway Hotel's head chef, Sean Abernethy.*

*Mayonnaise and potatoes:*

2 egg yolks

1 tsp Dijon mustard

500ml olive oil

Juice of half a lemon

500g new potatoes, scrubbed

2 small shallots, peeled, finely chopped

2 spring onions, trimmed, finely chopped

*Garlic butter:*

3 cloves of garlic, peeled, puréed

200g salted butter, softened

2 tbsp freshly chopped parsley

*Lobster:*

2 x 600g lobster

For the mayonnaise, whisk the yolks in a bowl and add the mustard. Gradually pour in half the oil (slowly – drop by drop – at first). Add the lemon juice and the rest of the oil, slowly, whisking constantly, until it reaches the desired consistency. Season to taste.

Cook the potatoes for 18-20 minutes until tender, then allow to cool and cut into quarters. Add the mayonnaise to potatoes, along with the finely diced shallots and spring onions.

For the garlic butter, mix the ingredients thoroughly.

For the lobsters, the hotel recommends popping each one in the freezer for an hour or so to put it to sleep then putting a sharp knife through the top of its head, to ensure it is killed instantly. After this they cut in half, remove the internal organs, and rinse thoroughly under cold water. (I prefer to half-cook/parboil the lobster before cutting in half. I would boil for 3 to 4 minutes – once the water has returned to the boil – then remove, cool, cut in half and proceed with the recipe.) Crack the claws with the end of a knife or similar. Place on a baking tray, and smother the flesh with plenty of the garlic butter.

Bake at 180C/350F/Gas 4 for 6 minutes (for a 600g lobster; longer if it is a larger one), and serve warm with the potato salad.

*Scalloway Hotel Lobster.*

# Mussels
## (Yell, Shetland)

Gordon Johnson is director of Shetland Select, the company that provides some of the best mussels in Scotland. Based in Basta Voe on the island of Yell, they have also recently started harvesting in Vementry off the west mainland of Shetland. The water depth, tidal flow and shelter are optimum in Shetland's 'voes' (small fjords). Water depth is important for mussels as the ropes must not touch the sea-bed or starfish climb up and feast! The tidal flow and shelter are crucial as the water is clean and unpolluted and there is just enough ebb and flow to ensure water purity, but the mussels can still cling on to the ropes without being carried away by the tide. What sets these mussels apart, Gordon told me, is the fact they are seasonal. When they are spawning, from the end of May or early June through to mid-August, they stop harvesting the mussels, to avoid them being contaminated with toxins in the water as temperatures increase during the summer.

The life cycle of a mussel is about three years and begins when the spat (young mussels) attach to the lines (which are hairy ropes), then after a year, these are transferred to the main growing ropes where they stay attached for some two years. Shetland's mussels are big and juicy and that is the market that Gordon's company targets. So they end up in Britain's' high-end restaurants, as well as the fish shops all over Shetland. The furthest they go is Beirut and Dubai, which seemed to me surprising until I was told that they can be harvested on the Sunday and, having been washed, graded and bagged, are then sent by truck and plane to arrive in the middle east by Wednesday at the latest.

Mussels are not an expensive product and people tend to forget that they are not only delicious and versatile, they are also a very healthy food: low in fat and cholesterol, they are high in Omega-3 fatty acids. But what marks Shetland Select's mussels apart from others is the seasonality. The taste is so good, they are worth the wait.

# WARM MUSSEL SALAD

*serves 2*

*To cook the mussels: wash the mussels under running water. If any mussels have cracked or broken shells, discard them. If any are slightly open, tap sharply, and if they do not close, again they should be discarded. Pour 100ml white wine or water into a deep pan, bring to the boil and tip in the washed mussels. Cover tightly and cook over a high heat for 3 to 4 minutes, shaking the pan a couple of times. Discard any that are not opened.*

*My Shetland friend Isabel Johnson always liked to serve Waas Bakery's Tattie Braed (Potato Bread) with any mussel dish.*

200g freshly cooked mussels, still warm

For the salad:

½ bulb of fennel, trimmed and very thinly sliced

½ red onion, peeled and very thinly sliced

A handful of rocket

For the dressing:

2 tbsp olive oil

1 tbsp fresh lemon juice

1 clove of garlic, peeled and chopped

1 tsp grain mustard

2 tbsp parsley, chopped

Mix everything for the salad together. Combine the dressing ingredients with some salt and pepper, then pour over the mussels. Tip this over the salad, toss gently and serve warm with some good bread.

*Opposite: Black Pudding Crostini.*

# 5
# Meat

# Lamb
## (Ronnie Eunson, Shetland)

Del the sheepdog bounds to the top of the hill at his master's command to round up the sheep. After several frantic zigzags around them, they end up in a line like dancing girls at the Folies Bergères, except in place of feathers there is wool. Lots of it. These Shetland sheep resemble the sheep young children draw: thin, spindly legs with a barrel-shaped load of wool on top. As the line approaches, Ronnie Eunson, who farms here at Uradale farm, continues to give Del his commands – 'Away back' – until the dog finally crouches down behind his charges.

The pure-bred native Shetland sheep, some 700 of them, reared on Ronnie's organic farm, graze on the fields that run from the hilltops right down to the sea. This ancient breed (neolithic sheep bones reveal its ancestry here) graze on heather grassland that might contain wild flowers and herbs such as wild thyme, violets, orchids, primroses or bird's foot trefoil. Seaweed is also a part of many of the Shetland sheep's diet. Ronnie Eunson explained to me how they somehow – innately – know when the tide is ebbing and that is when they come down to the shore to graze. The seaweed not only provides the animals with essential minerals (they only start going down to the shore at the end of the year when there is less grass), it gives an additional flavour to the meat, which has been proved to have unique health-giving properties.

Once Del has released the flock from his hypnotic gaze, the sheep bound back up the hill (I like to think, to enjoy the striking view over Clift Sound, south of Shetland's ancient capital, Scalloway, towards the island of Foula 25 miles to the west) and I quiz Ronnie about these unique health benefits. Studies some years ago found that the meat from the native Shetland breeds has high levels of CLA (conjugated linoleic acid), which has been shown to reduce the risk of cardiovascular disease and have an inhibiting effect on cancer growth. The lambs that are traditionally raised, fed on these heather pastures, show higher levels of omega-3 fatty acids than other sheep. The Shetland breed also had a healthier balance of omega-3 to omega-6 fatty acids than other breeds. All in all, once butchered, they are a mouthful of good health; and before that, gambolling around the fields like woolly dancing girls, they are a joy to behold!

As I sat in the Eunson farmhouse discussing native sheep, Ronnie tells me about the cold mutton (roasted but still pink and moist) and bere bannocks he took to a UK Slow Food AGM and how much everyone loved them. In Ronnie's words, people are voting with their tastebuds. His meat is so good, it needs very little in the way of add-ons when cooking, but the older it gets the more spices and flavourings can be used to complement the strong flavour of what becomes mutton. He now has his son Jakob working with him; as a trained butcher, he butchers all Ronnie's meat, ready for sale.

Uradale Farm is also home to a herd of native Shetland cattle which, like the sheep, roam over a wide area and eat a diverse diet. Ronnie has about 100 head of cattle and, just like his sheep, the native cattle are smaller than non-native. Ronnie's native cattle will weigh in at about 230kg as a carcass; non-native breeds are some 100kg heavier. The Shetland beef is sold primarily over Shetland, into the best restaurants and outlets such as Lerwick's speciality food shop, Scoop, and the Scalloway Hotel.

His lambs, sold in Edinburgh and London, are at least five months old, sold between the end of August and early January. Shetland lamb also now has the P.D.O. (Protected Designation of Origin) status which Ronnie reckons is welcome because the native products have something very special to offer the marketplace. It is a richly flavoured meat, the taste described by Edinburgh butcher Sandy Crombie as 'rather like tasting very good malt whiskies from different areas; it absorbs everything from the area and embodies it'. This native lamb with its long pedigree is not only healthy, its flavour is unsurpassed. Shetland lamb is a taste of both land and sea.

# BRAISED SHOULDER OF SHETLAND LAMB WITH ANCHOVIES AND ROSEMARY

*serves 6*

*This is a wonderful slow-braised lamb recipe that comes with its own gravy. And do not be put off by the anchovies; they simply add a gloriously savoury tang to the dish. Serve with roast potatoes and a green vegetable. Most Shetland lamb shoulders are boned and rolled and so if you are using a boned shoulder, just reduce the cooking time accordingly; cook for about an hour and a half for the first timing and then for about 20 minutes longer.*

2 tbsp extra-virgin olive oil

Whole shoulder of lamb on the bone, approx. 1.8 kg

2 fat garlic cloves, peeled and chopped

2–3 stalks of rosemary, leaves removed, and chopped

100ml red wine vinegar

6–8 anchovy fillets, finely snipped

Heat the oil in a large casserole dish and brown the meat all over. Remove the meat and add the garlic and rosemary to the dish. Stir well and add the vinegar. Bubble on a high heat for a minute or so, then add 150ml of cold water and bring to the boil. Season, then return the meat to the pan. Baste and cover: either with a lid not quite firmly on, or with a sheet of double foil leaving a couple of inches uncovered. The space allows the liquid to evaporate.

Place in a preheated oven (180C/350F/Gas 4) for about 2 hours, basting a couple of times. Then remove the cover and add the anchovies to the liquid, stir well (they dissolve into the sauce) and return to the oven. Increase the heat to 200C/400F/Gas 6 for a further 30 minutes, or until the lamb is tender and the sauce bubbling. Stir and taste the sauce, seasoning to taste if necessary. Carve and serve with sauce and vegetables.

*Lamb on Shetland.*

# ANN JOHNSON'S SHETLAND SHORT RIB

*serves 6*

*This recipe is based on one from Ann Johnson whose food emporium Scoop in Lerwick is known all over the islands for the diversity of its products, but mainly for the way Ann champions all quality Shetland produce. She sells Ronnie Eunson's native beef and lamb and has superb vegetables and salad leaves from Turriefield Vegetables in Sandness, in the far west of mainland Shetland. Regular bags of kail, cabbage, spinach, beetroot, rocket and fresh herbs are sold at Scoop, as well as local oatcakes and bread from Waas bakery in Walls and Da Kitchen bakery in Yell. She also has delicious hand-baked cakes and pies from German Katya, whose apple pies are some of the best I have ever tasted. Ann's recipe using Uradale Farm native beef is delicious.*

2 tbsp olive oil

2kg short beef ribs

2 large onions, peeled and sliced

6 carrots, peeled and chopped

4 garlic cloves, peeled and finely chopped

A good knob of fresh ginger (3–4cm), peeled and finely chopped

2 x 400g cans chopped tomatoes

400ml beef stock

Heat the oil in a deep casserole, brown the beef all over and remove to a plate. Add the onions, carrots, garlic and ginger and sauté till softened, adding a splash more oil if necessary. Return the beef to the pan, add the tomatoes, stock and salt and pepper, then cover tightly and cook at 150C/300F/Gas 2 for about two and a half hours, until you can see the beef slipping off the bone. Check the seasoning before serving with mashed potatoes and a green vegetable.

# Black Pudding
## (Stornoway)

In Arthur Herman's book *The Scottish Enlightenment*, there is a description of the Highlands in the early 1700s and the deprivation of the typical Highlander, particularly in winter. 'Highlanders often had to bleed their cattle, mixing the blood with oatmeal and frying it on the fire. Sometimes cows were bled so frequently they could barely stand.' This is similar to the ritual certain African tribesmen, such as the Suri or Masai, continue, bleeding their cattle directly into a vessel to drink the warm, almost coagulating, blood 'fresh'. At least the old Scots cooked theirs with oatmeal, as a primitive type of black pudding. But, thank goodness, nowadays when black pudding is made, the beast is no longer sentient.

After a hearty Hebridean breakfast of porridge and black pudding, perhaps only the serious black-pudding lover would want to see the latter being made. But since I was in Stornoway and just along the road from Charles Macleod, producers of some of the best black pudding in the land, it certainly made sense to a pudding fanatic like me.

Round the back of the butchers shop where fabulous Hebridean lamb and venison are sold alongside the long, fat rolls of various puddings (black, white, fruit), is a new production unit just for the puddings. When they began to produce black puddings for sale in outlets other than the shop, some four decades ago, they were producing 300 black pudding a week; now production has increased enormously and scarcely keeps up with demand: production can be up to 10,000 a week. For Stornoway black pudding is so well known and respected, it is synonymous with quality. And of course only the best ingredients are used to make this product that is both earthy yet sophisticated, homely yet stylish.

Stornoway Black Pudding was awarded PGI (Protected Geographical Indication) in 2013. This means it can only be produced if it is made in the town or within the parish of Stornoway. The most famous and arguably the best producer of Stornoway black pudding is Charles Macleod, the butchers opened in 1947 by the original Charley Barley. He was so-called from schooldays, since everyone on Lewis, or so it seems, was called Macleod. After his untimely death in 1967, sons Iain and Charles took over the business and built it up from tiny shop to a large premises that includes an extensive delicatessen and full mail-order facilities.

Now it is the sons' daughters – the original Charley Barley's granddaughters – who run everything. Charles' two daughters, Shona and Ria, and Iain's daughter Rona, are now fully in charge of this thriving family business. Shona runs operations and the production side of the puddings; Rona looks after finances and quality management, including food hygiene; and Ria runs the shop. Rona's sister Claire helps out with PR and HR. It is not only unusual for a women-only team to run such a successful family business, but for three such young women to be doing so. They are all in their thirties, but having grown up surrounded by the other family members working for the business, it seemed only natural for them to assume the mantle themselves. Charles – Shona and Ria's father – used to run the family farm on Lewis till his death in 2015; Iain – Rona's father – was in charge of running the shop. Now all three young women are in charge of not only the shop and website sales but also the production of some of the best black pudding in the world. Of the eight directors of the company, six are women, including Rona, Shona and Ria. This is a sign of progress and modernity that also extends to the black pudding production.

However it is changed days from when most crofts made their own 'marag dhubh' (Gaelic for black pudding) after a sheep was killed, nowadays sheep's blood is not used. But there is still a distinctive Hebridean taste to Stornoway black pudding, whether it is eaten in the Western Isles or in a chic London restaurant. Perhaps not everyone shares my curiosity to see it being made, but once tasted, whether at breakfast or tea, it is never forgotten. To make the pudding, Rona showed me how the ingredients – dried blood, suet (which they cut by hand to ensure a good flavour, but without the visible globs of fat characteristic of English and French puddings), oatmeal and onions – are mixed with the spices, which include salt and pepper. The spicing is the same since production started in 1947 and this is still a family secret. The ingredients are mixed together, placed in the hopper, encased in the 'skins', then hung in loops on racks and cooked. The regular long rolls cook for three hours, the smaller ones for two and a half hours. Then they are chilled down in the chilling room and packed and sent all over the country. With such high standards and delicious taste, it is hardly surprising this black pudding has won several Gold Medals at the Guild of Fine Foods Great Taste Awards over the past few years.

Though most people in the Western Isles, just like elsewhere in mainland Scotland, confine black pudding to the breakfast table, there are more and more cooks serving it up for lunch and dinner. Shona Macleod likes to stuff mushrooms with it, dip them in a garlicky batter then deep-fries until crunchy, tempura-style. Or she serves it on one of her Granny Jessie's famous pancakes, with bacon and scallops (known as clams locally), and with a drizzle of maple syrup. Rona likes it as a stuffing for roast chicken.

I like to serve it with bacon on a tattie scone, with tomatoes in a savoury tart, with pork in a hearty casserole; or grilled and clamped into a morning roll with a runny fried egg. Black pudding has come out of the breakfast closet and is now very much on lunch and dinner tables across the land.

# TRADITIONAL HEBRIDEAN BLACK PUDDING

*makes one large pudding*

*This recipe is from a cookbook,* The Modern Crofters Cookbook, *in the Great Bernera Museum, originally compiled by residents of Bernera to raise funds for their community hall. This also has a recipe for a white raisin pudding (sometimes known as fruit pudding), made by mixing flour, raisins, sugar and suet to fill a cleaned intestine and boiling for a couple of hours.*

*I have reproduced the black pudding recipe here, with the quantities unchanged from the book in pints and pounds, as I fear no-one is going to get their hands easily on three pints of fresh sheep's blood. I am including it now for its historical interest.*

*Still on the intestine theme, there is another interesting Hebridean dish, 'Snala'. To make this, the intestine of the sheep is turned inside out. After being thoroughly washed, it is stuffed with chopped kidneys, suet, oatmeal, blood and salt, then tied and boiled in a coil (snailshell) shape then fried before serving.*

| | |
|---|---|
| Sheep's intestine | ½lb oatmeal |
| 3 pints sheep's blood | 1lb chopped suet |
| 1lb chopped onion | |

Clean the intestine well and leave to soak overnight.

Using your fingers, stir the blood well to break up any lumps. Season, then add the onion, oatmeal and suet.

Fill the intestine with the mixture, sew up the ends and boil in a pan of boiling water for about 2 hours.

# MUSHROOM RISOTTO WITH BLACK PUDDING AND TRUFFLE OIL

*serves 4*

*Mushrooms and truffle oil are a match made in heaven, and mushrooms work well with black pudding. Perhaps unsurprisingly, then, the three marry well too. Take your time with this risotto, stirring patiently until the rice has absorbed just enough stock to become cooked but not stodgy; it should always have a little bite.*

Approx. 900ml chicken stock

60g butter

1 small onion, peeled and chopped

300g risotto rice (Arborio or carnaroli)

100ml dry white wine

2 tbsp extra virgin olive oil

4–8 slices Stornoway black pudding

200g chestnut mushrooms, chopped

2 heaped tbsp parmesan cheese, grated

2 heaped tbsp freshly chopped parsley

Truffle oil

Bring the stock to a simmer and keep hot.

Heat half the butter in a large pan and cook the onion until soft. Add the rice, stir until coated and then add the wine, cooking until evaporated. Add the hot stock ladle by ladle, stirring, only adding another ladle once the previous one has been absorbed. You may not need all the stock; cook till the rice is al dente.

Meanwhile, heat 2 tbsp of oil in a frying pan, cook the mushrooms, remove with a slotted spoon and keep warm. Add the black pudding and fry over a brisk heat till crispy and cooked through. Remove to a plate lined with kitchen paper and pat off any excess fat.

Remove the risotto from the heat, stir in the parmesan and then the remaining butter. Cover, leave to stand for 5 minutes, stir in the parsley and taste for seasoning.

To serve, ladle the risotto into warm shallow bowls. Top each bowlful with some mushrooms, then a slice or two of black pudding and finally a shake or two of truffle oil.

*Black Pudding Crostini.*

# BLACK PUDDING CROSTINI
## *makes 12*

*The crostini are made by toasting small rounds of good bread, preferably Italian. You can do this well in advance and keep them in an airtight container.*

2 slices of Stornoway black pudding, cut into quarters

Extra-virgin olive oil

2–3 tomatoes, diced

Black olive paste, optional

12 crostini

Basil leaves, optional

Fry the black pudding in 1 tbsp olive oil until crispy and cooked through.

Mix the tomatoes with a couple of tbsp oil and some freshly milled black pepper and sea salt.

To assemble, place the crostini on a board, spread with olive paste if you like; top with the black pudding and tomatoes and serve warm, with a scattering of basil leaves if you like.

# STORNOWAY SCOTCH EGGS
## *makes 12*

*This is Harris-based chef Chris Loye's stunning creation, which he often serves as canapés at his pop-up restaurant on the west coast of Harris. He serves with a beetroot-flavoured mayonnaise, but also suggests one zapped with some wholegrain mustard instead.*

12 local quail eggs

250g Stornoway black pudding

4 large eggs, whisked gently

100g flour

300g fresh breadcrumbs

Oil, to deep-fry

To serve:

100g mayonnaise

1 tbsp wholegrain mustard

Boil a pan of water, add the quail eggs and continue to boil for 1 minute 45 seconds for white shell and for 2 minutes if the shell is speckled. Remove the eggs, refresh in cold water and peel the shells gently before fully cold to ensure the shell comes off easily.

Chop the black pudding and put in a food processor to blitz briefly.

Add a little of the whisked eggs to the black pudding, enough to bind it.

Place a layer of clingfilm on top of a chopping board. Spread the black pudding mix on top thinly, cover with another layer of clingfilm and roll out evenly until it is around 2-3mm thick. Peel the top layer off and cut enough black pudding mixture to cover an egg, around 5cm (don't worry if it is too small, you can always add more).

Dry off the eggs, taking care not to burst them. Cover in the black pudding and repeat until all the eggs are done.

Put the flour in a tray and the remaining whisked eggs in another tray. Then coat the black pudding-covered egg with the flour and roll in the whisked egg. Add 6 at a time into the breadcrumbs, ensuring they are fully coated, then repeat for the next 6 eggs.

Now repeat the egg wash and breadcrumbs step again for all 12 eggs (no need for flour this second time).

Whisk the mustard into the mayonnaise, ensuring it is mixed well and no lumps remain.

After being coated in the breadcrumbs twice, the eggs are ready to cook. Deep fry at 180C/350F for about 2 minutes, until golden-brown.

To serve, cut the eggs down the middle to expose the runny yolk and sit them on the mayonnaise to ensure they stay in place.

# STORNOWAY BLACK PUDDING CHEESE SCONES
### makes 10

*This recipe was inspired by Isle of Lewis baker Mairi Ord's Twitter post of 'marag' (Gaelic for black pudding), apple and sage scones. Like me, Mairi favours using Stornoway black pudding.*

*I like the black pudding just with cheese. Eat warm with a dod of butter – with soup or, if you make them very small, as canapés, split and topped with a smear of tapenade and a dice of tomato*

*Stornoway Black Pudding Cheese Scones.*

*Unless you want the entire dough to look grey, ensure the black pudding is chilled before you dice and then fold in gently so that the small pieces do not break up.*

| | |
|---|---|
| 450g plain flour | 200g black pudding, skin removed, diced |
| 2 rounded tbsp baking powder | 2 large free-range eggs |
| 125g butter, cubed | Whole milk |
| 175g grated mature Cheddar (I like Isle of Mull) | |

Sift the flour and baking powder into a large bowl and rub in the butter. Stir in the cheese, add a pinch of salt and, folding in very gently, the black pudding.

Place the eggs in a measuring jug, stir lightly then add enough milk to make up to 300ml (about 150ml). Stir lightly, then add most of this to the mix (enough to make a softish dough), and gently combine with floured hands. Bring together gently (you do not need to knead, only bring the dough together) and place on a floured surface. Pat out till about 3cm high. Using a fluted cutter, cut out 10 large scones and place on a lightly buttered baking tray.

Brush the tops with any liquid left in the jug (add a splash more milk if necessary) and bake near the top of a preheated oven (220C/425F, gas 8) for about 12 minutes or until golden and well-risen.

Remove to a wire rack and leave until barely warm before splitting and spreading with butter.

# Beef
# (Luing)

The Luing breed was developed by the Cadzow brothers on the island of Luing in Argyll off the west coast of Scotland. Luing is easily reached by a short ferry service over the Cuan Sound from the island of Seil, which is now linked to the mainland by the famous Clachan Bridge. Slate was the principal industry on Luing and was still being quarried here till the 1960s. Now livestock farming is the principal activity, in particular the unique herd of beef cattle bred by the island's owners over 70 years ago.

In 1947, having admired the outstanding complementary qualities of two great beef

*Cattle on Luing.*

breeds – the Beef Shorthorn with its good fleshing (capacity to fatten) qualities and the Highland with its ruggedness and hardiness – the Cadzows selected some of the best first cross Shorthorn/Highland heifers available. The Highland heifers were bred to Shorthorn bulls and by following this up with line-breeding, the Luing breed was firmly established, with many generations sired by Luing bulls. The British Government officially recognised the Luing as a breed in its own right in 1965.

The second and third generation of Cadzows now live on the splendid estate at Ardlarach on the south west of the six-mile long island. Their house up on the hill overlooking the Sound of Luing has panoramic views over to the islands of Lunga and Scarba. Shane Cadzow and his wife Tooti and their three grown-up children, Kate, Archie and Jack, farm the island with the Luing progeny of the original breed of cattle and also farm sheep, mainly blackface ewes crossed with Lleyns and/or Texel tups.

When you visit Luing you cannot help but notice the cattle and sheep seem to have free range across the entire island, and within their family groups they more or less do. It's this family system that allows for the longevity of a pedigree herd like this on Luing. It is sustainable and fully accountable – and provides delicious beef. This rugged breed continues to be part of the stunning landscape of this picturesque island.

There is a wonderful collective of island bakers on Luing, which has two main villages, Toberonochy and Cullipool, and the group supplies baking for the village shop and café on the island. From shortbread to lemon drizzle cake and flapjacks, they provide excellent baking for locals and visitors alike. The island of Luing is not dependent solely on the beef to give the island its excellent reputation in culinary circles.

# Tooti Cadzow's recipe for Luing Beef Fillet with Salsa

*serves 10*

For the beef:

2kg fillet of beef

Olive oil

A knob of butter

For the salsa:

6 medium tomatoes peeled, seeded and chopped

A large bunch of fresh coriander and mint, finely chopped

3 cloves of garlic, peeled and finely chopped

2 small red onions, finely chopped.

2 red birds eye chilli, finely chopped (if you don't want the salsa too hot use one and remove the seeds)

2 ripe avocados, chopped into large chunks

30ml fish sauce

60ml balsamic vinegar

175ml olive oil

2 tsp Dijon mustard

2 limes, the grated zest and juice

Prepare the fillet by removing all the sinew and season with lots of pepper and salt to taste. If it is to be eaten cold, cook earlier on to save hassle, and if to be eaten hot, the preparatory stage of browning the meat can all be done earlier in in the day. Pan fry with some olive oil and the butter in a very hot frying pan to seal it, until brown, about 5 minutes in all; do not overdo it but put aside in an oven dish until you want to complete the cooking. If cooking soon, leave at room temperature; if cooking later in the day, keep in a chilled place.

When it is time to cook, place in a preheated oven (200C/400F/Gas 6) for 10 minutes per kilo for blue rare and then leave to rest for 10 minutes on the carving board. Add an extra 5 minutes for rare and another 5 minutes for medium rare, another 5 for medium.

For the salsa, mix all the ingredients together ahead of time, but make sure it's out of the fridge for two hours before serving, either heaped by the side of the sliced beef or in a serving bowl alongside.

# Mull Haggis

Jeanette Cutlack is one of the few haggis makers in the Hebrides. She began making it a few years ago from her home at Ballygown near Torloisk, overlooking the Isle of Ulva, when her son's school was hosting a Burns lunch. She offered to give it a try. Having worked in commercial kitchens in the past, she thought it would not be too difficult; she soon realised haggis-making is a challenge! But, ever one to embrace new skills, she thought she might as well give it a go. It went down well and so she resolved to continue, perfecting it as no-one on the island made it. Thankfully, Mull has its own slaughterhouse so getting hold of the ingredients did not prove hard.

Since then, Jeanette has changed and developed the recipe through trial and error and sheer determination to make it work. The haggis is made with sheep's offal and beef suet, both of which come from the local slaughterhouse. Though haggis recipes vary, she uses primarily lungs and some hearts but tends not to use liver (unless there is a shortage of lungs and hearts) as it can give the haggis quite a dense texture. I agree that liver does not always make for a pleasing mouthful in a haggis. Jeanette's Isle of Mull haggis has a wonderful, true, clean taste that is perfectly spiced. When she began, she was making some dozen haggis a week but now she is struggling to keep up with demand, as she has orders for around fifty a week in the summer season.

She is surrounded by supportive neighbours and friends who wanted to see her do well, and now she sells her haggis in many shops around the island.

In 2014, she set up a small restaurant in her house, open six days a week in the summer and then only for private functions over the winter. This forced her to come up with different ways of serving her haggis as most guests want to try it. She is also given suggestions from friends and diners. One diner of Moroccan descent suggested a haggis pastilla (haggis, chopped apricots, almonds and cinnamon baked in filo) which turned out to be a success. Another variation is an eastern European pirozhki, a bun made with an enriched dough, stuffed with braised cabbage and haggis (of course), then deep fried. In general, Jeanette likes to team up the haggis with something sweet, for example haggis, pork and rowanberry jelly sausage roll. She mostly uses artificial casing to enclose the haggis but for Burns Night she uses natural casing so that there is the full drama of stabbing through the skin at the appointed line of the *Address to the Haggis*:

> 'His knife see rustic Labour dight,
> An cut you up wi ready slight,

Trenching your gushing entrails bright,
Like onie ditch;
And then, O what a glorious sight,
Warm-reekin, rich!'

There is a recipe for 'haggas pudding' from the early eighteenth century that is not dissimilar to today's method of making haggis; it is made by boiling lamb lights, heart and kidneys, shredding the meat and mixing with beef suet. Then currants, nutmeg, 'sweet herbs', eggs and cream are added, before being seasoned and boiled in a paunch. The haggis has a long and proud tradition.

# MULL HAGGIS PASTILLA
*serves 4*

3 sheets filo pastry (approx. 30cm long)

50g butter, melted

I haggis (450–500g)

I small onion, peeled and finely chopped

I tsp honey

I tsp ras el hanout

75ml lamb stock or hot water

50g chopped apricots (or dates)

A pinch of chilli powder,

I tbsp tomato puree,

The zest of one orange

I tbsp flaked almonds

A small pinch of ground cinnamon and I tsp icing sugar, to decorate

Brush the filo pastry with melted butter and layer one sheet on top of another.

Mix the haggis and the next 8 ingredients together and place the mixture in the centre of the layered filo sheets; bring up the edges so that the mixture is enclosed. Flip it over and lay on a flat greased baking tray or a 20cm cake tin and sprinkle some flaked almonds on it. (At this stage, you can chill overnight if baking the next day.) Bake in a preheated oven (200C/400F/Gas 6) for about 20 minutes until golden brown. Sieve the cinnamon and icing sugar over the top and serve at once, with a couscous salad.

*Opposite: Mull Haggis Pastilla.*

# Mull Beef
## (Glengorm Estate)

Glengorm Estate on Mull has some 60 breeding cows and, depending on the season, the number of young stock can be between 150 and 250. These are pure Highland cattle – the cute little ones with the thick shaggy hair and long curved horns. The Highland bulls (there are three 'senior' bulls and two yearlings) are even more magnificent, with their stocky build and larger girth.

Tom Nelson, owner of Glengorm Castle and farm manager, tells me he also has some 750 blackface sheep, so their lamb (more hogget than lamb as it is one to two years old) is also for sale, along with the wild venison shot on the estate. But it is the cattle I am here to find out about.

Highland cattle are the oldest pedigree breed of cattle in the world. Originally there were two types of Highland cattle. The ones known as Kyloe were small and black in colour and were associated with the west of Scotland and the islands, whereas the larger red-haired type grazed in the Highlands. Today they are known collectively as Highland cattle and the recognised colours are Red, Black, Yellow, Dun, White Brindle and Silver.

Highland cattle are robust and able to withstand the long harsh winters that are common in the Highlands. Due to the rugged nature of their native habitat, the cattle eat plants that other cattle avoid, therefore making the most of poor forage and an economic contribution to hill and upland areas.

They do not need to be housed in the winter because nature has provided them with a weatherproof shaggy coat and an extra thick hide. Highland beef tends to be leaner than most because, unusually for cattle, they get most of their insulation from their trademark thick shaggy coat rather than from subcutaneous fat.

The life-cycle of the Highland cow starts in secret. Highland cows like to give birth in private, and so when their time is near, they leave the main herd and go in search of a secluded spot. Most calves are born on the hill without assistance. Their young are born ready clothed in their warm insulating coats, ready to face the cold, wet and snow.

Once the calves are born, the mothers keep them secluded, in a safe place – behaviour which is similar to that of deer and antelope, where the young are deposited somewhere between periods of suckling, to keep predators away. Tom tells me that by law, cattle have to be ear-tagged within seven days after birth and so because of this, it is important that new calves are located. Farmers can sometimes spend days trying to locate these calves to tag them!

One of the many wonderful aspects of this beef is that Highland cattle are slow-maturing and only killed at three to four years, much later than most breeds. They are kept outside for most of their lives and finished on grass and heather on the hills. Then, since Mull is fortunate to have its own abattoir, there is a mere 30-minute journey to the final stage, where the beast is killed and butchered.

The meat of Highland beef is dense and dark in colour. It is tender and well marbled and is both healthy and nutritious, with a lower level of fat and cholesterol and a higher protein and iron content than other beef. Tom's Glengorm beef is available all over Mull in restaurants and shops and also, since the family own the Tobermory Bakery, the beef is converted into delicious meat pies. Made from quality local beef, these are worth making the long trip over on the ferry from Oban. Highland beef is a treat worth seeking out.

# TOM NELSON'S SPICY BEEF SOUP

*serves 6*

*This is one of Tom's favourite recipes using his excellent Highland beef. It is more thin stew than soup. He likes to use stewing or shin beef, diced.*

| | |
|---|---|
| 1 onion, peeled and chopped | 1 red chilli, trimmed and finely chopped |
| 2 fat carrots, peeled and chopped | 1kg diced beef |
| 2 red peppers, trimmed and chopped | 2 dessertspoonfuls of curry paste |
| 1 fat courgette, trimmed and chopped | 2 x 400g tins of chopped tomatoes |
| Olive oil | 2 dessertspoonfuls of tomato purée |
| 4 garlic cloves, peeled and finely chopped | 1 litre beef stock |
| A 2.5cm chunk of fresh ginger, peeled and finely chopped | Sour cream and fresh coriander, to serve |

Sauté the first four ingredients in a little oil in a large heavy saucepan (or casserole dish with lid), then add the garlic, ginger and chilli and continue to sauté gently for a minute. Remove with a slotted spoon and add the beef, in batches, using a little more oil. Season with salt and pepper. Brown the meat then remove it with a slotted spoon. Add the curry paste to the pan (and a dash more oil if necessary) and cook for 1–2 minutes. Return the sautéed vegetables, beef, tomatoes, purée and stock. Bring to the boil, stir well and reduce to a low simmer, cover and cook slowly over a very low heat for about 3 hours.

Season to taste and serve in bowls with a dollop of sour cream and some fresh coriander.

# ISLAND MINCE AND TATTIES WITH OR WITHOUT MEALIE PUDDING

*serves 4*

*It would once have seemed not only strange but perhaps also insulting to have to give a recipe for Mince and Tatties, a classic Scottish dish. But nowadays since mince is used more often in Bolognese sauce or chilli con carne, it is perhaps good to remind ourselves how tasty and wholesome it is. In some rural parts of Scotland and the islands, a white (mealie) pudding is placed over the mince as it cooks; in Aberdeenshire it is called Mince and Mealies. I prefer to heat up the white pudding alongside the mince.*

*My mum's basic recipe for mince was to brown the mince in a little dripping, add chopped onion and water and simmer until cooked. She thickened it at the end with Bisto, but her mother used a product called 'Burdall's Gravy Salt' which is now virtually impossible to buy. Instead of Bisto I use a good beef stock cube; and a teaspoon of marmite also adds a good savoury flavour. A shake of Worcestershire sauce at the end is not traditional but my family likes it. Mushroom ketchup was added to the minced collops of last century and early this century, so if you can find this, you can also add a few shakes. It is important to use a solid reliable pan; my Granny Ward always used a black cast-iron pot to make her mince.*

*The good flavour comes from only the best-quality mince, preferably steak minced in front of you at your butchers. I made a pot of mince from Isle of Luing beef and it was divine, so full of flavour. The texture should be soft enough to dribble seductively over your mound of mash, but thick enough to make a decent forkful.*

Dripping or butter

1kg best beef mince

1 medium onion, peeled and very finely chopped

1 leek, cleaned and very finely chopped

3 carrots, peeled and very finely chopped

1 organic beef stock cube

Worcestershire sauce (or mushroom ketchup, optional)

Mashed tatties made from 4 large potatoes, boiled and mashed with plenty of butter

Heat a knob of hot dripping or butter in a heavy-based pan until hot, then brown the mince over a high heat, stirring around to break up the mince. This should take about 5 minutes.

Add the onion, leek and carrots, then mix the stock cube with 100ml boiling water and add to the mince, with some salt and pepper. Stir well then cover and cook over a medium heat for about 20 minutes until cooked.

Add a good few shakes of Worcestershire sauce or mushroom ketchup if required, then check the seasoning again. Serve piping hot with the tatties and some freshly cooked peas or stir-fried cabbage.

For 'Mince and Mealies', simply drop a couple of small white (mealie) puddings – whole – on top of the mince for the last 15 to 20 minutes or so of cooking. The pudding may burst, but this does not matter at all as it only improves the flavour of the mince.

# HEBRIDEAN LAMB SHANKS
# WITH ROSEMARY AND THYME

*serves 4*

*Whenever I am in Stornoway, I go to Charles Macleod the butchers and buy some lamb shanks to take home, they are so tasty. I usually cook them in this simple recipe, with rosemary and thyme. Though sometimes I go mad and add a cinnamon stick, some chopped apricots and serve scattered with pomegranate seeds and fresh mint.*

*If there are children eating this, I substitute the port with more lamb stock — so some 350ml of stock altogether.*

*I like to serve them with butterbean mash which I make by mashing potatoes with a drained can of butter beans, enriching it with some milk and a good glug of extra-virgin olive oil. Roast leeks or stir-fried cabbage is all you need to complete a comforting and truly tasty dish.*

| | |
|---|---|
| 4 fat lamb shanks | 2 sticks celery, chopped |
| 25g plain flour, seasoned | 1 fat parsnip, peeled and chopped into big chunks |
| 3 tbsp olive oil | |
| 1 onion, peeled and chopped | 2 fat carrots, peeled and chopped into big chunks |
| 3 garlic cloves, peeled and chopped | 100ml port plus 1 tbsp port |
| 2 leeks, cleaned and chopped | 250ml lamb stock, hot |
| 1 fennel bulb, trimmed and chopped | 2 sprigs each of thyme and rosemary |

Place the shanks in a large freezer bag with the seasoned flour and shake well to coat. Heat 2 tbsp of oil in a large casserole, and once hot, add the shanks and brown all over. Remove and add 1 tbsp oil. Gently fry the vegetables in the casserole, adding a little more oil if necessary.

Return the lamb to the casserole and add the port and the hot stock. Bring to the boil, add the thyme and rosemary, cover tightly and place in a preheated oven (150C/300F/Gas 2) for about 3 hours.

Remove as much of the liquid and the vegetables as possible, using a deep ladle, and place this in a food processor. Whizz until smooth then return to the pan with the lamb and 1 tbsp port. Taste and season and reheat to piping hot. Serve with mash and green vegetables.

*Hebridean ewe and lamb.*

# HEBRIDEAN ROAST LAMB

*serves 6–8*

*This recipe is from Hamish Taylor from Flodabay, eastern Harris. He says it is nothing new but is his family favourite. The final taste (and smell) of roast lamb is significantly influenced by what it has been fed on, according to Hamish: he finds that lamb raised on heather or heathland (part grass and part heather) is far tastier than lamb raised on grass alone.*

| | |
|---|---|
| 1 leg of lamb (whole or part) | Herbs such as rosemary, optional |
| Butter | |
| 2–3 onions, peeled and sliced | Choice of root vegetables for roasting alongside |
| A few garlic cloves, peeled and halved if thick | |

Sear the meat in a hot frying pan with a little butter. 'Stab' the meat with a knife in several places, and insert whole or part cloves of garlic in each stab. Season the meat as desired with pepper, salt and herbs.

Lay the lamb on the sliced onions in a roasting tin and cook in a pre-heated oven for 20 minutes per 450g plus 20 minutes at 180C/350F/Gas 4, basting occasionally.

Meanwhile, roast your root vegetables.

When cooked, remove the meat from the oven, cover with foil and let it rest while making your gravy, using the contents of the roasting tin as the base for this.

Carve and serve with roasted vegetables.

*Opposite: Stag on Lewis.*

# 6
# Game

# Venison
## (Raasay)

Raasay is a hidden gem in more ways than one. Geographically, it sits in the lee of its mighty neighbour, Skye. It is only about 12 miles long and has a population now of some 140 to 150 (though back in the day before the Clearances it was several hundreds) and is of significant geological interest, with most of the south of the island formed of Torridonian sandstone, the north of Lewisian gneiss.

And of course there is the poetry. One of the most important poets of the twentieth century, Sorley MacLean, was born and grew up here and, with his four brothers and two sisters, would recite poetry in Gaelic in the township of Osgaig (also written as Oskaig). Verses from his most well-known poem 'Hallaig' are inscribed on a plaque mounted on a cairn overlooking the deserted village of Hallaig. Like so many other villages and townships, this was abandoned during the nineteenth-century Clearances and the homes broken up. Much of the stone from these houses was used to build sheep enclosures and fanks for the many sheep that soon replaced the humans on the south of the island. The people were either sent to the barren grounds at the north of the island, or forced to emigrate. There are tales of the sound of mothers' weeping being heard across the sea from Raasay as the ships containing their sons and daughters set sail from Portree to Canada.

'Hallaig' begins: 'Time, the deer, is in the wood of Hallaig . . .'

As well as the sheep, deer have roamed for many years. Indeed, there is a school of thought that the meaning of Raasay in Gaelic is 'Roe Deer Island' but in fact there are two alternative etymologies: *Eilean Ratharsair*, Racing Water Island, and *Eilean Ratharsaidh*, Roe Deer Island. These are derived from Old Norse, *rás* meaning course or channel, and *rár* meaning roe deer. Since there are strong tidal currents between the island and Fladda, Eilean Tighe, Rona and Soay, it is more likely that it means Racing Water Island. Besides, the locals I spoke to cannot recall seeing a roe door for at least 50 years. Interestingly, James Boswell, during his visit to Raasay in 1773, remarks in his *Tour of the Hebrides* on 'the abundance of black cattle, sheep and goats' on the island. He then comments, 'There are no deer; but Raasay [the laird] told us he would get some.'

The wild red deer can be heard roaring throughout the rutting season as you walk around the gentle paths and steep slopes of the island. I took a walk from the end of Calum's Road, the road from Brochel to Arnish built almost single-handedly by islander Calum MacLeod, a feat that dominated the last 20 years of his life. The walk led through

*The Sorley MacLean memorial, Hallaig, Raasay.*

muddy cliff-top paths and slippery seaweed-covered rocks to the tidal island of Fladda. We passed the old schoolhouse of Torran to which children would walk every weekday, not only from Fladda but also from Rona up and over the hill, which was only reachable by boat, each carrying a burning peat in the winter to light their way through thick bracken and heather on the dark mornings and afternoons.

I spoke to a man born and bred on Raasay, John William Gillies, who knows all about the roaring of the deer. There are some 280 head of red deer now on the island. He and six other islanders have the shooting rights on Raasay; the seven of them form a committee for the Raasay Crofters Association who hold both shooting and fishing rights. The season for shooting the hinds is 21 October until 15 February and for the stags it is 1 July until 20 October. They are allowed by the Department of Agriculture to cull 18 stags and 18 hinds a year, and these are gralloched on the hill once shot. This procedure is to remove the guts, which would otherwise ferment.

*Holoman Island, Raasay.*

John makes a delicious casserole with the island venison which is butchered over on Skye then brought back to the village shop in Inverarish on the island and to Raasay House kitchen to be appreciated by visitors and locals alike.

He told me tales of deer, stags and hinds, swimming over the sea to the islands of Rona at the northern tip and to Scalpay off the south. (There is more than one Scalpay in the Hebrides; this one is south of Raasay; the other to the east of Harris.) They are wild animals, therefore travel all over the island on open, common grazing. As a crofter, he has sheep (the island has mainly Blackface but also some Cheviots) and also cattle (pure Shorthorn and cross with Limousin). The islanders rent out a bull which comes over from the mainland to Raasay for May to October. He told me a story of one perfect summer day years ago, he had taken the bull off the ferry in its halter and it was so unusually hot he had to stop at the shop for a bottle of lemonade. While inside, he tethered the bull outside the shop where you might leave a dog – or a pram. It was the talk of the island.

In the village school (which had six children on the roll when I was there) they know all about animal husbandry and the provenance of their food. The islanders also teach their children how to forecast the weather without going online. If the sheep are on the top of the hill, it is going to be a good day. The sheep will also stroll over to the tidal Holoman Island, which is very near John William's croft, if it's nice weather. If it is not fine weather, they will stay on the lower land or eat seaweed along the shore. Who needs weather forecasts when you have island sheep?

# JOHN WILLIAM'S RAASAY VENISON CASSEROLE

*serves 4*

*Serve with mashed potatoes and a green vegetable such as cabbage or kail.*

500g diced (stewing) venison

½ bottle of gutsy red wine

Olive oil

2 tbsp seasoned flour

1 large onion, peeled and chopped

1 fat leek, cleaned and sliced

2 large carrots, peeled and chopped

1 red pepper, deseeded and chopped into large chunks

1 x 400g tin of chopped tomatoes

Worcestershire sauce

A handful of chopped flat parsley

The night before, put the red wine over the venison and place in the fridge, covered, overnight. The next day, strain over a sieve and toss the meat with the flour in a large plastic bag.

Heat 1 tbsp of oil in a large casserole dish and brown the meat all over. Remove the meat, add another tbsp of oil, then gently sauté the onion, leek, carrot and pepper until softened. Now return the venison to the pan with the tomatoes and a good dash or three of Worcestershire sauce. Bring to the boil, remove from the heat and cover tightly.

Place in a preheated oven (100C/200F/Gas ½) and cook for anything between 6–8 hours. Stir every couple of hours and taste for seasoning, then add the parsley just before serving.

# VENISON STEAKS WITH BEETROOT AND HORSERADISH SAUCE

*serves 4*

*The sauce is a doddle to make and has the texture of a hummus or pesto rather than a thin sauce cooked in a pan. It can be made a day in advance. Then, about half an hour before serving, remove the venison from the fridge to come to room temperature before cooking. Cuts you can use are thicker pave, or thinner rump; if using the latter, it's even more important to undercook then rest the meat while still very pink, otherwise it becomes tough.*

*I like to serve this with clapshot and some broccoli or spinach.*

250g cooked beetroot, peeled and chopped

The grated zest of 1 small orange

2 heaped tsp horseradish sauce

50g freshly grated parmesan

Extra-virgin olive oil

4 Hebridean venison steaks (each about 150g)

For the sauce, place the first 4 ingredients in a food processor and whizz briefly, then add enough oil (5–6 tbsp) to form a thick paste. Season to taste and set aside.

Heat 2 tbsp oil in a frying pan to hot, add the steaks and season. Cook for 2 minutes, turn and continue to cook for a further 1–2 minutes before transferring to an ovenproof plate. Place in a low oven (150C/300F/Gas 2) for 10 minutes, then serve them atop a mound of clapshot and with a dollop of beetroot sauce on top.

# Venison
## (Jura)

Lizzie Massie's career as a much sought-after cook and chef goes back to her Hebridean roots. The natural larder on the island of Jura – from venison and sea trout to wood sorrel and blaeberries – has inspired her since her childhood there. Her great-grandfather Walter Hargreaves Brown bought Ardlussa House, in the north east of the island, from the Astor family in 1926. His daughter, Lizzie's grandmother Margaret, lived there after the Second World War to help her husband, Robin Fletcher, recuperate after some time in a Japanese prisoner-of-war camp. They decided to stay on and turned the estate into a working farm, and this continued until 1962 when Lizzie's grandfather died. After a spell living on the mainland in Comrie, Perthshire, Lizzie's family returned to Ardlussa in 1984 and have lived there ever since.

It was the most idyllic place to grow up. Lizzie remembers every summer going out in boats to collect crabs from the lobster pots; sometimes they sailed over to the west coast of Scotland and stayed overnight in caves. She remembers canoes and boats and trips to the beach; and always good, seasonal – if possible, local – food. And so, after finishing at university, she started cooking as a career, firstly at a shooting lodge, then in a Glasgow restaurant, then in Val d'Isère as a chalet cook, before cooking and teaching at the Edinburgh School of Food and Wine in Edinburgh. She ended up as chef for the First Minister at Bute House in Charlotte Square from 2011 until 2014.

Now she spends almost half the year on her beloved Jura, cooking for shooting parties and guests who can rent out half of Ardlussa House. Her menus always include as much local produce as possible: Jura venison, of course, and lamb from their own flock of Jacob lambs. Salmon and sea trout are also popular.

Ardlussa is only eight miles south of the remote farmhouse at Barnhill where George Orwell lived from 1946 until 1948; it is also where he wrote *Nineteen Eighty-Four*. The seclusion he revelled in has changed little – the population is now steady at only 200, far less than its busier neighbour Islay, with well over 3,000 inhabitants. Another unchanging feature, something that has remained the same over the centuries on Jura, is the wild deer population. Red deer have roamed on the island forever, the population now numbering some 5,000. The name Jura means Deer Island, derived from the Norse Gael era, from the Old Norse for deer. The accolade of being labelled Deer Island is also often given to Raasay, but since we know deer were only introduced to Raasay after James Boswell and Samuel Johnson's visit there in 1773, it seems that Jura trumps Raasay as there was never any need to import deer to Jura. They have simply always been there. Lizzie told me not only how superb Jura venison is, but how large and heavy the red deer are, some even weighing in at an astonishing 26 stone (165kg).

There are also wild goats on Jura, a legacy, it is said, from the Spanish Armada when some made it ashore from shipwrecked boats. Others – probably more sensibly – say that they are descendants from nineteenth-century crofters' goats. They are often seen down on the beach, grazing on seaweed. Lizzie has plans to cook them one day, but it would have to be a young goat; an old billy goat would be a little tough after even a long slow braise.

There is plenty to forage on Jura, including all sorts of seaweed. Lizzie uses wild mushrooms and wood sorrel in sauces, and rowan berries in jellies and to add a wonderfully fruity tang to game dishes. As well as using the island's whisky she also now adds an ingredient that is newer to the market, Lussa Gin, part-owned by three enterprising Jura women, one of whom happens to be her sister-in-law and who lives with Lizzie's brother and family in Ardlussa House. The gastronomic heritage of Ardlussa lives on.

# LIZZIE MASSIE'S VENISON CARPACCIO
*serves 8*

| | |
|---|---|
| 500g venison fillet | 1 tsp crushed juniper seeds. |
| 50ml Lussa Gin | *To serve:* |
| 50g caster sugar | 2 tbsp pickled beetroot, |
| 50g sea salt | thinly sliced |
| 2 tbsp chopped thyme | 2 handfuls rocket |

Place all the ingredients into a large bag with a good grinding of black pepper. Make sure the fillet is covered with the gin cure. Leave in the fridge for a couple of days, shaking the bag occasionally.

After a couple of days, bring the venison to room temperature and sear in a hot pan – roughly a minute for each side.

Once cooled it can be wrapped and placed in the freezer for a couple of hours; this can make it easier to slice.

Serve thinly sliced, with the beetroot and rocket.

*Jura.*

# VENISON SCOTCH EGG WITH JURA WHISKY MAYO

*makes 4 eggs, to serves 8 as a starter*

*This is another of Lizzie Massie's wonderful recipes using Jura venison.*

5 large free-range eggs

400g of either venison
  sausage meat or venison
  mince

2 tsp juniper berries, crushed

2 tsp thyme, chopped

100g plain flour

100g Panko breadcrumbs

Oil for frying

*To serve:*

Garden salad

4 tbsp mayonnaise

Jura whisky

First of all, place 4 of the eggs into a pan of boiling water and boil for 6½ minutes for runny, or 7½ minutes for a slightly harder yolk. Once boiled, place in a bowl of ice-cold water.

Mix the chopped juniper and thyme with a little seasoning in with the meat. Divide the mixture into four separate balls.

Peel the eggs once they have cooled. Flatten out the balls of meat (this is easier to do using clingfilm and a rolling pin). Wrap each flattened ball of meat round the eggs.

To breadcrumb, place the flour in a bowl; in a separate bowl crack in the remaining egg and beat. Put the breadcrumbs in another bowl. Place the meat-covered eggs, separately, in the flour, then the egg and then the breadcrumbs. Make sure they are all well covered.

Heat either a deep fat fryer, or a pan of oil, to 150C/300F. Place the eggs in and cook for 8–10 minutes.

Halve the finished eggs, once cool, and serve with some garden leaves and a tbsp of mayonnaise with a dash of Jura whisky mixed through.

# VENISON LASAGNE
### *serves 4-6*

*This is Flora Corbett's delicious lasagne which she makes from her family's Lochbuie Estate venison on the south of Mull.*

| | |
|---|---|
| 1 onion, peeled and finely chopped | 100ml milk |
| 1 carrot, peeled and finely chopped | 3 tbsp tomato purée |
| | 100ml white wine |
| 2 sticks of celery, trimmed and finely chopped | 300ml beef stock |
| | Fresh or dried lasagne |
| 200g streaky bacon, chopped | 900ml white sauce, flavoured with a little grated nutmeg |
| 1 tbsp olive oil | |
| 500g venison mince | 50g grated Parmesan cheese |

Sauté the onion, carrot, celery and bacon in the oil, increase the heat and add the mince. Once this is browned, pour in the milk, bring to the boil then reduce down until the milk is absorbed.

Add the tomato purée, wine and stock, stir well, lower the heat and simmer, covered, for as long as possible (Flora likes to do this stage for 45–50 minutes) then taste and season.

To assemble, layer up the mince, lasagne and sauce in a buttered lasagne dish, sprinkle Parmesan on the top. Bake for about 45 minutes at 180C/350F/Gas 4 until bubbling.

# Guga
## (Lewis)

Fisherman Dods Macfarlane has lived in the port of Ness on the Butt of Lewis in the Outer Hebrides all his life. For most of the year he sells fresh and salt herring, mackerel, smoked haddock, cod and ling. One day in the summer, however, he and nine other men of Ness sail to a remote rock in the Atlantic – Sula Sgeir, some 40 miles north of Lewis – to harvest guga, as part of a legacy that has existed for many centuries.

'The ile is full of wild fowls, and when the fowls has their birds ripe, men out of the parish of Ness in Lewis sail and tarry there seven or eight days and to fetch with them home their boatfull of dry wild fowls with wild fowl feathers.' This was written by Donald Monro, Archdeacon of the Isles in 1549. And ever since then, men from Ness on the northernmost tip of the Hebridean island of Lewis have ventured forth, often in atrocious conditions, to stay on Sula Sgeir and harvest the delicacy that is known as guga.

Gugas are plump young gannets, 2,000 of which are harvested every year. This is permitted because of a Statutory Order allowing the guga harvest inserted into the 1954 Protection of Birds Act which had made it illegal to harm gannets and other wild birds. Once the Nessmen arrive on the tiny island, they set up camp and spend 14 days catching the birds, which involves remarkable skills of rock-climbing, usually amid adverse weather conditions. Once killed the birds are decapitated, plucked, singed, de-winged and split open. They are then salted and piled in a 'pickling stack', a mound with a wheel formation.

All over the islands of Scotland, wild fowl have been harvested and eaten through the centuries, just as they have on other northerly islands such as the Faroe Islands. Seabirds and their eggs provided a reliable food source and records show that on islands from St Kilda and Mingulay to Copinsay in Orkney and Foula in Shetland, wild fowling was commonplace.

When I read about the St Kildans' tradition of boiling a puffin in with their oats to flavour their porridge, I was intrigued. I wondered how it might taste and whether or not this unusual cooking method was perpetuated once this most westerly and remote of Hebridean islands was evacuated in 1930. All sorts of seabirds were harvested there over the centuries, for their oil, feathers, their eggs and their flesh. In *An Isle called Hirte*, author Mary Harman records a visitor to the islands in 1842 enjoying 'a meal consisting of fulmar, auk, guillemot, one of each, boiled; two puffins, roasted; barley cakes, ewe-cheese and milk; and by way of dessert, raw dulse and roasted limpets.'

*Heather, Lewis.*

But I was keen to discover if, since 1930 and the end of St Kildan community, there was anywhere else in Scotland where such 'delicacies' were still consumed. Another visitor to the island in the mid-nineteenth century described the cooking methods: 'puffins were boiled sometimes in the breakfast porridge; and split dried puffins were propped before the fire and roasted.' This tradition was by no means unique to St Kilda. On the island of Lewis where some of the 36 St Kildan evacuees ended up, puffin consumption also took place: in the Lochs area of Lewis, south of Stornoway, it was a delicacy enjoyed by many. One local told me it was still eaten on Lewis until the 1960s.

On Tiree, I discovered from fisherman Iain Macdonald that cormorant was a staple of islanders there until the 1970s. But long before people could obtain a good supply of salt, the sea birds were air-dried, instead of being preserved by salting, and eaten throughout the winter. Shags, cormorants, puffins, fulmar, auk and gannet were eaten on the islands as regularly as mince and tatties were on the mainland of Scotland.

But back to the Men of Ness and the guga: when the men return home to Ness with their harvest, they are met on the quay by locals queueing to buy pairs of guga which will be desalinated, boiled and eaten with potatoes. Guga is one of Dods' favourite dishes – the taste often described as neither fish nor fowl, somewhere between steak and kipper. One year, Dods took a barbecue to Sula Sgeir, to much teasing from his fellow hunters. In the morning he marinated some guga in HP sauce before barbecuing it that night. Dods insists it was absolutely delicious.

The fishy taste of seabirds is primarily in the fat, and the regular method of simply boiling the fowl helps reduce it. Because of the salting of the guga in the 'pickling stack' it is important to soak it in cold water for a couple of days before cooking, changing the water regularly.

# GUGA AND TATTIES

*serves 6*

*Cold milk is the traditional drink to accompany this delicacy. I recommend a gutsy red wine, however, to ease down the unique and particular flavour and textures of the bird.*

*On the Faroe Islands, schnapps is the preferred drink to go with their baby gannet or fulmar, and something like this I would also recommend, the strong spirit helping cut through the greasy taste of the guga.*

*Unless you want the smell of guga all over your house, it is a good idea to cook it outside – in the shed or garden – otherwise the smell in your kitchen lingers for days . . . I say this from bitter experience!*

2 guga, washed well

Boiled potatoes in their
    jackets, to serve

Start a day or two before by soaking the guga in a bucket of cold water overnight, changing the water a couple of times, to remove as much salt as possible.

Then, on the day of cooking, cut each bird into 4 portions and wash again. Place in a pan of cold water (no salt) and bring to the boil. Simmer for 30 minutes, then tip off the water and refill with fresh cold water. Bring again to the boil and continue cooking for a further 30 minutes over a low heat, until done. (If the birds have been in brine for over 4 months, change the water twice. Dods reckons the birds are best after only 3 days in salt.)

Serve with boiled potatoes in their jackets.

*Raasay Distillery, looking over to Skye.*

Alasdair Day is co-founder of the fabulous new Raasay Distillery with its statement gold roof and views over to the Cuillin in Skye that are so majestic they take your breath away. The flavour of the whisky is lightly peated and fruity – which hopefully suits the animals on the island too, as the draff (a by-product of the ground-up malted barley used in the distilling process) is given to the local crofters to feed their livestock. The distillery is based at Borodale House, which used to be the estate manager's house for Raasay estate.

*Alasdair Day at the distillery.*

During their initial planning to open a distillery on Raasay, their biggest problem was finding a source for water, but after drilling just up the back of the site, they came across a well from Celtic times with a trace of mineral content in the water; the flavours of a light peatiness and fruitiness suit the minerality perfectly. Then came the equipment – beautiful copper stills from Italy – and the plan was on a roll. By autumn 2017 the distillery opened, with a launch whisky labelled While We Wait. This has the characteristics of their own make whisky which is in the barrels and ready for drinking by 2020.

As well as the whisky being excellent to drink on its own, it is superb in cocktails. Alasdair also suggests mixing with rose lemonade. And he loves to cook chicken with it.

# CHICKEN AND MUSHROOMS WITH RAASAY WHISKY SAUCE

*serves 2*

*Serve with new potatoes and a green vegetable such as broccoli, or asparagus in season.*

| | |
|---|---|
| 10g dried wild mushrooms (I like porcini) | 200g chestnut mushrooms, sliced |
| 2 free-range chicken breasts | 2 shallots, peeled and finely chopped |
| 1 level tbsp plain flour, seasoned | 60ml Raasay whisky |
| 2 tbsp olive oil | 200ml double cream |

First soak the dried mushrooms in about 100ml of boiling water, enough to cover, and leave for 20 minutes or so.

Toss the chicken in the flour and brown in a wide frying pan in 1 tbsp of olive oil. Remove after it is browned on each side and add the remaining oil and the chestnut mushrooms and shallots. Drain the wild mushrooms, reserving the liquor, and add them to the pan. Sauté gently till softened, then add the whisky, mushroom liquor and cream. Bring to the boil, then reduce the heat, add the chicken and cover with a lid. Cook for 10 to 12 minutes (depending on the thickness of the chicken), until the chicken is cooked through. Taste and season the sauce.

*Opposite: Rhubarb, Muckle Roe, Shetland.*

# 7
# Berries and Rhubarb

## Rhubarb
## (Fair Isle)

Florrie Stout and her husband Jimmie are sheep farmers on Fair Isle. But, like so many other islanders, they have secondary jobs such as crewing the mail boat or knitting the sweaters. And when I asked about car hire, Florrie said they do that too. Florrie told me all about food traditions in Fair Isle, especially about fruity puddings, lamb – and rhubarb.

Fruity pudding – not dissimilar to Scotland's cloutie dumpling – is boiled in the big stomach of a sheep and is primarily made from suet and dried fruit. Florrie says you need less suet as the stomach itself can be fatty. Nowadays, of course, no one makes these on the island, or the white puddings her mother-in-law used to make.

There is a very strong tradition of sheep farming in Fair Isle: the indigenous Shetland lamb is the one Florrie and Jimmy keep themselves, for their freezer, and the cross-breeds are sold on. The latter is a cross of Shetland, a smaller breed, with Texel, Cheviot or Suffolk. Fair Isle is famous for its jumpers, and so much of the wool from the sheep is made into the stunning jumpers that are thankfully now back in fashion. Fishing is also important to the islanders.

Rhubarb is important in Fair Isle, as it is in Shetland, and many gardens have a patch; when Florrie runs out in her own garden, she 'borrows' some from other islanders' gardens. Florrie always makes rhubarb jam and rhubarb tarts and crumbles.

# FLORRIE STOUT'S RHUBARB
# AND GINGER JAM
### makes 4 jars

*Florrie insists you should try to use new fresh rhubarb for this delicious jam, before it becomes stringy. The season begins in Fair Isle at the beginning of May. She says she prefers this recipe to the old-fashioned recipes which would have boiled the rhubarb for ages.*

1.1kg trimmed rhubarb, chopped (this is the trimmed weight)

1.1kg granulated sugar

Juice of 2 lemons

75g preserved ginger, finely chopped

Place the rhubarb in a large bowl in alternate layers with the sugar and lemon juice, cover and leave overnight. Next day, tip everything into a large preserving pan and bring to the boil, stirring, and boil rapidly for 10 minutes. It will rise to the top of the pan, so watch carefully all the time.

Add the preserved ginger, boil for a further 5 minutes and then test for setting by placing a few drops on a cold saucer: it will cool quickly. Push with your finger; if it wrinkles, it is ready.

Pot in warm, sterile jars.

# RHUBARB, HONEY AND OAT COBBLER

*serves 4–6*

*This delicious recipe was inspired by a recipe I saw in a magazine for rhubarb cooked with sugar and with an oaty cream topping. I have introduced honey and vanilla, both of which go so well with rhubarb. The result? Gloriously pink rhubarb cooked to spoon-tenderness with honey and vanilla, and topped with the crunchiest of oaty cobbles.*

| | |
|---|---|
| 500g young rhubarb, trimmed and chopped | 2 tsp vanilla extract |
| 4 tbsp runny honey | 150g whole rolled (jumbo) oats |
| 2 tbsp light muscovado sugar | 100ml double cream |

Place the rhubarb in an ovenproof dish with 2 tbsp each of honey, sugar and vanilla. Cover and bake in a preheated oven (180C/350F/Gas 4) for 20 minutes and remove.

Mix the oats with the remaining 2 tbsp honey and the cream. Spoon 6 spoonfuls of the oat mixture on top of the rhubarb in great blobs. Bake in a preheated oven, uncovered, for about 30 minutes until tender and crunchy golden on top. Serve warm with crème fraiche.

# RHUBARB CRUMBLE TRAYBAKE
## makes 12 squares

*This is delicious served warm with ice-cream for pudding; or cold with
a warming cup of tea from a thermos on a windswept Hebridean beach.*

500g rhubarb, washed and
chopped (this is the
trimmed weight)

75g light muscovado sugar

*For the base:*

75g ground almonds

175g self raising flour

75g light muscovado sugar

110g butter, chilled, chopped

1 medium free-range egg

*For the crumble:*

2 heaped tbsp oats

2 tbsp plain flour

3 tbsp demerara sugar

1 heaped tsp ground
cinnamon

2 tbsp sunflower oil

Cook the rhubarb with the sugar either in a pan over a very low heat or in a microwave.
A microwave will take some 5–10 minutes; a pan about 10 minutes once the sugar has
dissolved. Shake the pan from time to time to prevent sticking. Allow to cool and strain
over a sieve (but don't throw away the juices – I like to pour these over porridge or yoghurt).

For the base, place the first 4 ingredients in a food processor and process until
blended, then add the egg through the feeder tube and blitz briefly. Tip this into a buttered
20cm square cake tin, pressing the mixture down to make it level. Top with the cooled
rhubarb, leaving a border around the edges.

Combine the first 3 ingredients for the crumble, stir in the oil and spoon this on top
of the rhubarb, pressing down a little. Bake in a preheated oven (180C/350F/Gas 4) for
about 45 minutes until golden brown. Cover loosely with foil for the last 10 minutes if it
looks too brown.

Leave to cool completely before cutting into squares.

# BLUEBERRY GRUNT
*serves 6*

*There are blueberries being grown on the islands now and these are being widely used in the kitchens of restaurants there. In Edinbane, in the north of Skye, there are particularly good blueberries grown commercially by Skye Berries which are used in The Three Chimneys kitchen by chef Scott Davies, mainly in desserts but also in savoury dishes. Other Skye kitchens using these fabulous local blueberries are Kinloch Lodge and Sligachan Hotel.*

*This is a blueberry grunt, my version of an old Canadian recipe for a blueberry pudding topped with sweet dumplings. Imagine a tightly-lidded saucepan of berries and dumplings steaming away gently, with a reassuring, muffled 'phut' resounding occasionally from within, and you will begin to understand the etymology of the name. Since I am not partial to sweet dumplings, however, I have made the topping for the blueberries as more of a scone crust and baked it in the oven. Pedants among you might call it a cobbler, but I happen to like the word grunt. So, Blueberry Grunt it is.*

*Serve with thick cream or Greek yoghurt.*

| | |
|---|---|
| 600g blueberries | 1 level tsp baking powder |
| 100g golden caster sugar | Zest of 1 lemon |
| 2 level tsp cornflour | 50g butter, diced |
| 3 tbsp lemon juice | 1 medium egg, beaten |
| 175g self-raising flour | 4 tbsp milk |

Place the berries in a saucepan with 50g of the sugar. Dissolve the cornflour in the lemon juice and add to the pan. Bring very slowly to the boil. Boil for about 2 minutes until the juices are released, then remove from the heat and tip everything into a shallow oven dish.

Sift the flour and baking powder into a bowl and stir in the remaining 50g of sugar and the lemon zest. Rub in the butter, then stir in the egg and milk to form a soft dough. Drop 6 spoonfuls of the dough over the top of the blueberries – they do not need to be too shapely as they will spread out haphazardly during cooking. Bake in a preheated oven (220C/425F/Gas 7) for about 20 minutes until the topping is golden brown and firm. Serve warm.

# BRAMBLE, APPLE AND BLUEBERRY HAZELNUT CRUMBLE

*serves 6*

*This is a pudding to be made in late summer and early autumn after scouring the hedgerows for brambles. You can get ahead with this pudding by making the crumble mixture several days in advance, tipping into a freezer bag and freezing until the day you need to use it.*

2 large cooking apples, peeled, chopped

Juice of half a lemon

50g caster sugar

450g brambles

200g blueberries

*For the crumble:*

125g plain flour

50g porridge oats

125g butter, chopped

50g chopped toasted hazelnuts

75g dark muscovado and caster sugars, mixed

First cook the apples for a few minutes in a saucepan with the lemon juice, sugar and a tbsp or so of water, until the apples are beginning to soften. Remove from the heat and tip everything into an ovenproof dish, then top with the brambles and berries.

For the crumble, mix the flour and oats and rub in the butter. Stir in the nuts and sugars. Tip over the fruit in the dish and pat down gently. Bake at 200C/400F/Gas 6 for 35 to 40 minutes until the topping is golden brown, the juices erupt up the sides of the dish and the smell is so enticing, you can wait no longer. Serve warm (not hot!) with crème fraiche, ice-cream or custard.

*Opposite: Bakery on Luing.*

8

# Baking

# Baking
# (Luing)

On the beautiful island of Luing off the west coast, there are 15 locals who run a collective of voluntary home-bakers to provide cakes for the Atlantic Island Centre in Cullipool, the largest village, and also the island shop. The baking group comprises 14 women and 1 man; 15 bakers out of a population of only 162 is rather remarkable. They provide cakes and traybakes all year for the island shop and the Atlantic Centre. They also provide bakes for the weekly community lunch club (a mere £3 for homemade soup, rolls and sandwiches) which is held at the Centre out of high season, and in Toberonochy Village Hall during the busy summer season. The bread they use is from Mary Braithwate who runs the wonderful Luing Bakery, where she bakes superb bread.

One of the volunteer bakers is matriarch Jane Maclachlan, who has two daughters and two granddaughters in the baking group too. The Maclachlan family have been on Luing since the 1700s and many of the family still live there, in Cullipool and Toberonochy, as well as on neighbouring Seil. One of Jane's sons is a fisherman on the island, landing langoustines and scallops from nearby waters. Fishing – and tourism – have taken over from the main industry on the island, slate, which was hugely important over the centuries, until 1965, when the last remaining island quarry was closed. Along with Seil and Easdale, Luing's slate industry was so important, it was said that these islands 'roofed the world'.

*Lemon Oat Bars.*

Jane's daughter Fiona's favourite recipe within the baking group is courgette and lime cake; Jane herself bakes shortbread, oatie biscuits and Victoria sponge.

Here are a couple of favourite recipes from Mary Whitmore who, with her husband Martin, helps run the baking collective; both are very fine bakers themselves. She is often seen leaving their house, which is on the shore near the Seil ferry, with a carful of bakes. Luing might be a small island, but it is big on cake!

# LEMON OAT BARS
*makes 12*

*Martin Whitmore, one of the Luing island bakers, makes this recipe at least once a week for the Atlantic Centre in Cullipool. It is one of the Centre's most popular bakes.*

| | |
|---|---|
| *For the crumble:* | ¼ teaspoon salt |
| 160g plain flour | *For the filling:* |
| 100g porridge oats | 1 x 397g tin condensed milk |
| 110g light brown sugar | 3 lemons, zested and juiced |
| 136g unsalted butter | |
| ¼ teaspoon bicarbonate of soda | |

Make the crumble by mixing the flour, oats, butter, sugar, bicarbonate of soda and salt in a food processor until just combined, or rub in by hand.

Tip half of the crumble into the baking tin (a square deep baking tin 20cm square, lined so it comes up two sides for easy removal of the bake once cooked) then press down firmly and bake at 190C/375F/Gas 5 for 10 minutes until golden and set.

Make the filling by mixing the condensed milk with the lemon zest and lemon juice until thickened. Spread the filling over the baked base. Carefully sprinkle over the remaining crumble and press down lightly. Bake for a further 20 minutes until the edges are golden brown and the centre is set but soft. Leave to cool completely before removing from the tin and cutting into 4 rows by 3 rows.

# BANANA CAKE WITH CHOCOLATE ICING

*serves 8*

*This is one of Mary Whitmore's most popular bakes for the Luing bakers; it is a moist and quite delicious cake that keeps well. Mary suggests freezing any overripe bananas (skin on; remove skin when almost thawed) and when you have three then you can make this cake.*

*I like to add half a teaspoon of freshly crushed cardamom to the cake batter, as the spice works so well with both banana and chocolate.*

For the cake:

250g mashed banana (about 3 bananas)

1 tbsp lemon juice

175g butter, slightly softened

300g golden caster sugar

3 large free-range eggs

1 tsp vanilla extract

300g plain flour

½ tsp salt

½ tsp bicarbonate of soda

1 tsp baking powder

160ml milk

For the icing:

35g dark chocolate (min 70% cocoa solids), roughly chopped

75g butter, softened

135g icing sugar, sifted

½ tsp vanilla extract

A drop of milk if necessary

Chocolate curls, to decorate

Beat the bananas with the lemon juice until mashed.

In a large bowl, beat together the butter, sugar, eggs and vanilla. Sift the flour and add the salt, bicarbonate of soda and baking powder. Stir this into the butter mixture. Add the milk, lemon juice and bananas. Beat well.

Divide the mixture between two x 20cm/7in round cake tins, the bases lined and sides buttered very lightly. Bake at 180C/350F/Gas 4 for about 35 to 40 minutes or till a wooden skewer comes out clean.

To make the icing, put the roughly chopped chocolate into a flat bowl and leave on an Aga to melt, or if, like me, you don't have an Aga, melt in the microwave.

Cream the butter and sugar, add the melted chocolate and the vanilla extract and mix well. If it's too stiff, add a bit of milk. Spread half between the cakes, and the other half on top.

Scatter a few chocolate curls on top to finish it off.

# Baking
# (South Skye)

Laura Rankin, who lives on the south west coastline of Skye at Ostaig, has baked for local cafés for a couple of years now. In Broadford she supplies Deli Gusta and An Crubh café on the way to Isle Ornsay. Laura is an extremely talented self-taught baker whose repertoire does not stop at simple sponge cake and scones. Her baking is modern, contemporary and utterly delicious; her cakes are not only baked, they are also served raw.

One of her specialities is a raw vegan cheesecake that is flavoured with local brambles from Tarskavaig. This is particularly popular with tourists and locals alike with allergies or who are vegans. Her apple rhubarb cake is a joy to behold – and to eat! It is made with apples and rhubarb from her husband Graeme's mum Rosie's garden in Achnacloich. The eggs she uses in her baked cakes are also local, from Tarskavaig.

*Laura, baker on Skye.*

Laura lived in Western Australia for a year and it was there she tasted raw cheesecakes and carrot cakes, which she adored. They are proving a big hit on Skye, as is this gorgeous apple, rhubarb and ginger cake.

# RHUBARB, APPLE AND GINGER CAKE
### serves 10

*Laura's mother-in-law, Rosie MacDonald, grows the rhubarb in her garden for Laura's wonderful creations. It is better with new season young pink rhubarb.*

300g self-raising flour

A pinch of baking powder

220g caster sugar

200g butter, unsalted, softened

3 medium free-range eggs

2 tbsp agave syrup or runny honey

200g rhubarb, chopped

200g cooking apple, chopped

2 balls of stem ginger, finely chopped

*Ginger buttercream:*

500g icing sugar

250g butter, softened

3 tbsp stem ginger syrup

1 tsp ground ginger

*Optional toppings:*

Stewed rhubarb and caramelised apple slices

Preheat your oven to 180C/350F/Gas 4. Grease and line the bottom of two 20cm round cake tins and set aside.

Sift the flour and baking powder together twice and set aside.

Cream the sugar and butter together for at least 3 minutes until smooth. Whisk in the eggs, one at a time, mixing well after each addition, and add the agave syrup or honey. Gently fold in the sifted flour and baking powder, along with the rhubarb, apple and ginger, ensuring it is well mixed throughout.

Divide the mixture evenly between two cake tins and bake in the centre of the oven for 30 to 35 minutes. When cooked, a skewer inserted into the centre of the cake should come out clean. Leave to cool in cake tins on a cooling rack.

*Laura's Rhubarb, Apple and Ginger Cake.*

Meanwhile, to make the buttercream, sift the icing sugar and ground ginger, add to the butter and cream together and add in the syrup.

Once the cakes are cooled, assemble by icing one with ginger buttercream, sandwich together and ice the top of your cake. Decorate your cake with stewed rhubarb and caramelised apples if using.

# RAW BRAMBLE CHEESECAKE

*serves 3*

*Laura uses local brambles, hand-picked near Tarskavaig. Instead of weighing out measurements, she says it is easier to use cups, so this recipe is given in cups, each measuring 250ml.*

*For the crust:*

¾ cup of almonds or mixed nuts, raw

⅔ cup of coconut chips, raw

4 soft medjool dates, pitted

1 tbsp coconut oil, melted

1 tbsp agave or maple syrup

*For the filling:*

2 cups of brambles plus extra to decorate

1 cup of cashews, pre-soaked overnight and strained*

4 tbsp lemon Juice

3 tbsp agave or maple syrup

1 tsp vanilla extract

⅓ cup of coconut oil, melted

coconut chips/flakes to decorate

Process the crust ingredients, except for the agave or maple syrup, in a high-powered blender until a sticky crumble is formed. Add the agave or maple syrup and blend until combined.

Transfer the crust mixture to either a 13cm springform pan or divide evenly into 3 x 10cm individual deep cupcake moulds, press the mixture firmly down and place them in the freezer while you are working on the filling.

Blend all the filling ingredients except for the coconut chips in a high-powered blender until extremely smooth. Remove the pan(s) from the freezer and pour the mixture over the crust. smooth off the top. Freeze overnight.

Decorate with brambles and raw coconut chips before serving. Allow the cake to thaw out to a softer consistency. (Keep leftovers frozen and thaw out before devouring them.)

*To pre-soak the cashew nuts, place in a glass bowl, cover with water and leave to soak for at least 4 hours or overnight in the fridge. Strain and discard the water. The purpose of soaking nuts is to rehydrate them and plump them up for blending into a smooth consistency.

# Cloutie Dumpling

Wherever you travel on the islands cloutie (usually written as clootie, but always known in my family as cloutie!) dumpling is made for celebrations such as birthdays, weddings and Christmas. There are many variations, including adding marmalade or carrot, or soaking the fruit in tea. This is my version of many island recipes, and is easy to make. But you do need an extra-large cotton cloth or tea-towel. Most modern tea-towels are too small; I bought three huge ones when my mum's old clout gave up the ghost – and they do the job very nicely.

Moist, rich and fruity, a good dumpling must have the characteristic skin: beware skinless clouties, as they are not authentic. The skin must be dried off before serving and this is done nowadays in the oven. But my mother tells me her task as youngest child was to dry off the dumpling in front of the open fireplace. She would sit there on a stool for 15 to 20 minutes, turning the dumpling round and round until it was dried off and ready to eat. I remember a cloutie dumpling being made by my Granny Anderson for birthdays and at New Year, according to Dundee tradition. But it was not only served on special occasions in in my parents' home-town; clouties in the Inner and the Outer Hebrides were served for birthdays and, just like the Dundee ones, studded with sixpenny pieces

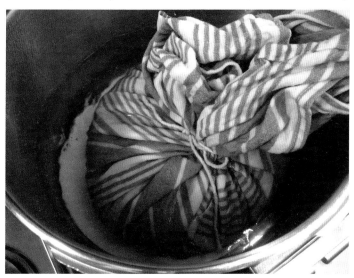

*The Cloutie in the pan.*

wrapped in greaseproof paper. On the islands, they are also made for other celebrations such as weddings. At a recent Tiree family wedding, the 'cake' comprised six cloutie dumplings!

Though cloutie dumpling is usually eaten hot, soon after it has been cooked, with custard, or with a cup of tea as a hot cake, it is also fried in bacon fat and served for breakfast. However, the most common way of eating cloutie dumpling on Tiree (and this is not as common on nearby Mull or in Dundee), is cold, cut into slices, then into fingers like a fruit cake. It is usually spread with butter, the latter being very important to the crofting communities which still thrive there. Freshly-churned butter on a slice of cloutie on Tiree is another example of certain foods being the perfect embodiment of the place. On Islay, it is one of cook Catriona McGillvary's specialities; she makes them not only for the Gaelic College café – served cold with coffee or tea – they are served as puddings at the many weddings and ceilidhs she provides clouties for, all over the island.

On the islands I have had the cloutie served hot with custard or fried with bacon. But, since my visit to Tiree, I have quite taken to eating it cold, not always daintily sliced or even with butter; sometimes, I am ashamed to say, torn off in inelegant clumps. As ever, the simplest foods taste best. On the island of Great Bernera, the traditional cloutie dumpling recipe is similar to mine below but, instead of 1 teaspoon of mixed spice, has 2 teaspoons of cinnamon and 1 teaspoon of ginger. It also uses golden syrup instead of my black treacle. The latter gives a darker colour.

If you want to add coins, wrap 5 pence pieces or charms in waxed or greaseproof paper and add to the mixture.

# CLOUTIE DUMPLING

*serves 8*

| | |
|---|---|
| 200g self-raising flour, sifted | 300g mixed dried fruit (sultanas, currants, raisins) |
| 150g fresh brown breadcrumbs | 2 tbsp black treacle |
| 200g shredded suet | About 300ml full-cream milk |
| 1 tsp bicarbonate of soda | Flour and caster sugar, to sprinkle |
| 2 tsp mixed spice | |
| 125g light muscovado sugar | |

*The Cloutie ready to serve.*

Mix the first 9 ingredients together in a bowl with a pinch of salt, adding a little more milk if necessary to get the correct consistency: you want a stiff yet dropping consistency.

Dip a large pudding cloth (or large tea-towel) into boiling water to scald, drain well using rubber gloves to squeeze it dry, and lay it out flat on a board. Sprinkle with flour and then sugar (I use my flour and sugar shakers): you want an even – but not thick – sprinkling. This forms the characteristic skin.

Spoon the mixture into the centre of the cloth, draw the corners of the cloth together and tie up securely with string, allowing a little room for expansion. Place the cloutie on a heatproof plate in the bottom of a large saucepan. Top up with boiling water to just cover the pudding (it must come at least three-quarters way up the side of the pan, leaving the string out of the water), cover with a lid and simmer gently for about three hours. Check the water level occasionally and top up if necessary. You should continually hear the reassuring, gentle shuddering phut, phut, sound of the plate on the bottom of the pan for the entire duration of cooking.

Wearing rubber gloves, remove the pudding from the pan, dip briefly into a bowl of cold water (for no more than 10 seconds) so the skin does not stick to the cloth, then lift the dumpling into a colander in the sink. Cut the string, untie the cloth and invert the dumpling onto an ovenproof plate.

Place in the oven (180C/350F/Gas 4) for about 10 minutes to dry off the skin – it should feel a little less sticky – then sprinkle with caster sugar and serve hot with custard, or cold with a cup of tea.

# BEREMEAL SHORTBREAD

*makes 24 pieces*

*I love the addition of some beremeal to a buttery shortbread. It adds a deep, slightly earthy edge – and good colour – to a basic shortbread recipe. It is also very versatile. You can roll the dough out thinly and cut into little round shortbread biscuits; if you do this, they will take only 25 minutes to bake.*

*I usually prefer the ease of tipping everything into a baking tin, then cutting into bars or squares. You can use caster sugar instead of icing sugar and plain flour instead of self-raising, but I like the lightness that comes with the combination of icing sugar and self-raising, to counteract any potential heaviness of the beremeal.*

250g butter, softened to room temperature

150g icing sugar, sifted

250g self-raising flour

100g beremeal

Caster sugar, to dredge

Place the butter and sugar in a food mixer and cream them together until pale. Once well amalgamated, add the flours, a good pinch of salt and continue to blend briefly, just until they are thoroughly combined. It might not come together, so you simply need to bring it together with your hands. Tip into a buttered Swiss-roll tin (23 x 33cm) and, using floured hands, press down so it is level on top. Prick all over.

Bake at 150C/300F/Gas 2 for 35 to 40 minutes. What you are looking for is a uniform golden all over.

Remove and dredge all over with caster sugar, and cut into squares or bars, while still warm. Leave for 10 minutes or so, then carefully decant onto a wire rack to cool.

For 'Alfajores' (Argentian shortbread toffee 'sandwiches' that I adored when I was in Buenos Aires), make the shortbread into little round biscuits instead of in a Swiss-roll tin, then, once cool, sandwich two together with a thin layer of dulce de leche (a thick caramel now available in the UK in tins), gently press together and roll the sides in desiccated coconut. You will need about 4 tablespoons of dulce de leche and about 100g of desiccated coconut.

For Beremeal Peanut Butter Shortbread Sandwiches, make the shortbread into little round biscuits. Once cool, sandwich them together with a peanut butter filling, made by combining 75g of butter with 300g sifted icing sugar and 2 heaped tablespoons of smooth peanut butter and enough milk (a tablespoon or 2) to combine into a stiff mixture that is soft enough to spread on the delicate biscuits without breaking them.

# STICKY APPLE CAKE
*serves 8–10*

*This cake is both easy and versatile, one of my family favourites, and since it keeps well, it is ideal to take on holidays to the islands. I remember a family picnic on Luskentyre beach on Harris with the wind howling and the cold air swirling around us as we crouched down among the dunes. A thermos of coffee and a slice of this cake, though, and everything seemed better. The sun even came out afterwards.*

*You can throw in a handful of chopped walnuts or pecans to the basic mixture; you can also replace one apple with a large ripe pear. You can substitute light muscovado sugar for the dark to give more of a light toffee flavour than a dark treacle toffee taste. It can be served cold with a cup of tea; or warm as pudding with crème fraiche or ice-cream. It's delicious – and versatile.*

3 medium free-range eggs

200ml sunflower oil

300g golden caster sugar

375g plain flour

1 tsp bicarbonate of soda

1 tsp ground cinnamon

2 tsp vanilla extract

2 large Bramley apples,
    peeled and chopped

100g dark muscovado sugar

3 tbsp whole milk

100g butter

Whisk together the eggs, oil, caster sugar and 50ml cold water in a bowl till thoroughly combined and smooth, then sift in the next 3 ingredients with a pinch of salt and stir well. Add the vanilla and apples. Pour the mixture into a buttered, deep 24cm loose-bottom cake tin. Bake in a preheated oven (180C/350F/Gas 4) for 50 to 60 minutes; test by inserting a skewer into the middle – it should come out clean. Cover loosely with foil towards the end, if necessary.

Meanwhile, place the last 3 ingredients in a saucepan and bring slowly to the boil. Boil for 3 to 4 minutes until thickened, stirring often. Cool for at least 5 minutes.

Once the cake has cooked, remove from the oven. Slowly pour over the sauce and return to the oven for a further 3 to 4 minutes, until bubbling. Remove to a wire rack and run a knife around the edges. Allow to cool in the tin before taking it out and cutting.

# SHORTBREAD CRUMBLE SLICE
*makes 20 slices*

*Based on one of New Zealand's wonderful traybakes, Tan Slice, this has a vanilla shortbread base, a layer of sticky toffee and a crunchy crumble topping. Delicious, and perfect for an island picnic on the beach, whether huddled in sweaters behind a windbreak with a thermos of hot coffee – or lying on the clean white sand in shorts, watching the cows stroll along the shore on a sun-kissed warm day.*

| | |
|---|---|
| 250g butter, at room temperature | For the filling: |
| 100g golden caster sugar | 75g butter |
| 1 tsp pure vanilla extract | 1 tbsp golden syrup |
| 400g plain flour | 200g (half a can) condensed milk |

For the shortbread, cream the butter and sugar together until light, then add the vanilla and flour. Combine well and press two-thirds of the mixture into a buttered Swiss-roll tin (23 x 33cm), pressing down all over with the palms of your hands until even. Prick lightly with a fork.

Meanwhile, heat all the filling ingredients in a pan on a low heat, stirring all the time until the butter is melted. Continuing to stir, let it bubble away for a couple of minutes, then pour the filling all over the base.

Crumble the remaining mixture evenly over the top and bake in a preheated oven (180C/350F/Gas 4) for about 25 minutes or until golden brown all over. Remove from the oven and cut into slices while still warm, then allow to cool before removing from the tin.

# FRUIT BANNOCK

*serves 12*

*This is not a usual Northern Isles bannock like a beremeal bannock; nor is it a Hebridean bannock which can be more like an oatcake. It is a big bulging sweet enriched bread, not dissimilar to a Selkirk Bannock but also resembling the fruit puddings often seen in butchers across the Hebrides. Alongside the black and white puddings hang fruit puddings, which are fried alongside breakfast bacon or served as pudding with custard.*

*My bannock is served cold, thickly smeared with butter. It is a joy to behold.*

| | |
|---|---|
| 1kg strong white flour | Grated zest of 1 small orange |
| 175g butter, softened | Approx. 500ml milk and water mixed, hand-hot (tepid) |
| 2 x 7g sachets of easy-bake fast-action dried yeast | |
| 75g caster sugar | 1 free-range egg yolk, beaten, to glaze |
| 350g sultanas/raisins | |

Sift the flour and a pinch of salt into a bowl, and rub in the butter till thoroughly combined. Stir in the yeast and sugar and add the dried fruit and orange zest.

Now add enough of the tepid liquid to combine to a firm but not sticky dough. Bring together with lightly floured hands, turn onto a floured board and knead well for 10 minutes or so until smooth.

Place in a lightly floured bowl, cover and leave somewhere fairly warm for one and a half to two hours, or until well-risen. (I leave on a wire rack a couple of inches above my gently heated kitchen floor.)

Knock down the dough and shape into a bannock: a round flattened dome about 28cm diameter. Place on a buttered baking sheet and brush all over with half the egg yolk. Return to the fairly warm place and cover with a large inverted bowl (of a size that is not going to impede further rising) and leave for about an hour, or until well-risen. Now re-brush with yolk and bake at 220C/425F/Gas 7 for 10 minutes, then cover loosely with a foil dome to prevent any fruit that is poking out becoming burned, reduce to 200C/400F/Gas 6 and continue to bake for about 30 minutes. It is ready once it is golden brown all over and the base sounds hollow when tapped underneath. Leave to cool on a wire rack, and once it is completely cold, slice and spread with butter.

# Baking
## (Great Bernera)

When I heard from my friend Maggie about her mother-in-law's memories of time spent with family on Great Bernera, an island off the west coast of Lewis, linked to the mainland by a bridge constructed in 1953, I was intrigued. Not so much by the simple foods they cooked – broth, home-made jams, fish such as mackerel or ling and home-made crowdie cheese – but it was the baking that fascinated me. Maggie's husband's granny and aunties used only their hands to bake. Whether it was cakes or scones, no wooden spoon would be used; only their hands. Alistair's Auntie Nessie's Lancashire Nuts (similar to custard creams) and Auntie Morag's cakes were legendary – and all prepared only by hand.

All the women on the island would make drop scones (also known as scotch pancakes); in the days when folk would just 'pop in', a batter could be rustled up as guests were stepping over the doorway and slapped onto the girdle as the guests settled into their seats by the fire. Anna Darling's (née Maclean) father was a baker from Ness on the north of Lewis who worked in Stag Bakery in Stornoway, so baking was important to the family. There was an old bakery in the village where Maggie and Alistair have their blackhouse on Great Bernera, but sadly it is many years since this functioned.

Maggie talked to Great Bernera crofter Finlay Maciver about being brought up as part of a large family on Great Bernera. He and his wife Cathy returned from working in Glasgow to bring up their own family on the island.

Finlay remembers the excitement of the island children when high tides in the summer would wash dulse onto the shore. It was, he says, a great treat, eaten a bit like children elsewhere ate raw rhubarb. The word would go out that there was dulse and the small island's children would run to the shoreline to gather as much as small arms could carry.

Finlay recalls growing up in a house with no electricity – it didn't come to the island until later than mainland Scotland – with candles and oil lamps for light and a pot hanging over the fire in which stews and soups would be tended. His mother was a good cook but there was nothing fancy about the food put on the table for hungry mouths: 'We would have lamb stews, barley soups, oatcakes,' he said. 'But there were no fancy implements. Our mothers made everything by hand – mixing cakes, and bread with their fingers.'

*On Great Bernera.*

Cathy, a retired community nurse, explained that it was sense more than measurement that was needed in cooking: 'Our mothers would feel the texture of the cake or bread or oatcakes and would throw in a dash of this, a handful of that.'

There was then fish aplenty – herring of course. But the Great Bernera islanders could be choosy. Mackerel was regarded as a bottom-feeder, therefore was not as popular as white fish.

Great Bernera women, just like the women all over the Outer Hebrides, made their own black pudding – '*marag dubh*' – using oatmeal and sheep's blood. Cathy recalls her father arriving home and being asked whether he'd got the blood from the slaughterhouse. Shamefaced, he admitted he'd left the big bottle of blood behind on the bus.

'*Ceann cropaig*' was another treat – fish livers mashed together with oatmeal and onions and cooked in a fish head. It was boiled in the pot over the fire for about half an hour and served with tatties, as was always the island way.

The population of the island is now more stable since the bridge was built, and many more tourists now visit, after the discovery of an Iron Age village in the north of Great Bernera. In 1993 a great winter storm reconfigured the beach at Bostadh, revealing stonework in the sand dunes where gradually eroding middens had long been observed. Eventually this threatened site was excavated in 1996, and a series of well-preserved houses, some virtually intact, were unearthed. Four houses were found, although there is the possibility that the village had once extended right across the present beach. The main settlement was occupied between the sixth to the ninth centuries AD, during the late Iron Age. It comprised a cluster of semi-sunken circular or cellular buildings, each with a rectangular central hearth and at least one smaller chamber opposite the main entrance.

The wide range of finds gives a picture of the lifestyle of the villagers, who lived by mixed farming, fishing, hunting and collecting seafood and seabirds. They would have fished for saithe, pollack, ling, whiting, flounder, herring and haddock. They kept cattle and sheep and cultivated beremeal to make simple bannocks and breads. They would also have had hazelnuts and crowberries in their diet. The Vikings then lived on the island from the ninth century AD, and further excavations found that a Viking house had been built over the site, from which the name 'Bostadh' (meaning farm in Old Norse) is presumably derived. The site was re-occupied in more recent times, with villagers living in Hebridean blackhouses until a scarcity of fuel forced the village to be abandoned in 1875. The remains of many of these abandoned blackhouses can be seen around Bostadh.

And the baking for which Great Bernera is so famous was done in the blackhouses on a girdle hung by a swee over a peat fire; later when kitchens had ovens, the women would have continued to bake, using their hands – and not implements like wooden spoons – to provide the daily fare of pancakes, biscuits and cakes. It is part of their heritage.

# TOFFEE ALMOND CAKE
*serves 10*

*This is one of Maggie Darling's favourite cakes and one that she enjoys baking while staying at their blackhouse on Great Bernera, where there is more down-time to relax.*

*The cake is delicious cold with tea or coffee – but can also be served barely warm for pudding, with perhaps some thick cream and some berries.*

| | |
|---|---|
| 150g butter, softened | For the topping: |
| 150g caster sugar (preferably golden) | 100g butter |
| | 100g demerara sugar |
| Zest of 1 large lemon | 100g flaked almonds |
| 2 large free-range eggs | 2 tbsp double cream |
| 100g self-raising flour | 1 heaped tbsp plain flour |

For the cake, cream the butter and sugar together until light and fluffy, then add the lemon zest and a pinch of salt. Add the eggs, a little at a time, incorporating a small amount of the weighed flour with each egg. Then fold in the remaining flour. Tip this into a buttered, square 24cm cake tin, base-lined with greaseproof paper. Place in a preheated oven (150C/300F/Gas 2) while you prepare the topping.

For the topping, melt the butter and add the remaining ingredients, stirring while it comes to the boil. Boil for a couple of minutes and remove from the heat.

Once the cake has baked for 20 minutes, remove from the oven and pour the topping over slowly, in stages. Don't worry if it sinks to the base in parts. It will all sort itself out.

Return to the oven and continue to bake for a further 30–35 minutes or until golden brown and firm to the touch. Run a knife gently around the edges, then allow to cool for about 30 minutes before decanting.

# CARROT CAKE
*serves 8*

*This recipe is from Careen MacLennan of Kirkibost, Great Bernera. She cooks and bakes for the Great Bernera Museum Café and many of the recipes she develops are based on her Bernera family's own traditional ones. This one goes down very well with the Museum Café visitors.*

4 tbsp vegetable oil (Careen uses corn oil)

225g caster sugar

3 medium free-range eggs

225g finely grated carrots

175g plain flour

1½ tsp baking powder

1½ tsp bicarbonate of soda

1½ tsp ground cinnamon

½ tsp salt

50g chopped walnuts

50g sultanas

*For the topping:*

100g cream cheese

50g butter, softened

1 tsp vanilla extract

225g icing sugar, sifted

For the cake, beat the oil and sugar together, then add the eggs one at a time.

Add the carrots, flour and other ingredients, and once well combined, tip into a buttered, base-lined 20cm round cake tin. Bake at 180C/350F/Gas 4 for about 1 hour. When tested with a skewer, it should come out clean.

Beat all the topping ingredients together, and once the cake is cool, slice it in half and sandwich the halves together with one half of the topping; spread the other half over the top of the cake.

# BARLEY BREAD
*makes 1 loaf*

*This is one of many interesting traditional recipes featured in the cookbook from the Great Bernera Museum, A Modern Crofters Cookbook. In keeping with the fact that most cooks on the island used measurements which were very vague, they often refer only to cups for measures and knobs of butter instead of weight. A breakfast cup is a regular teacup, not a coffee mug.*

*This is the Hebridean equivalent of Orcadian beremeal bannocks; beremeal can be used, but I would use half beremeal, half plain flour, as beremeal has a far stronger flavour than barley flour.*

| | |
|---|---|
| 1 breakfast cup of barley meal/flour | A knob of butter |
| ½ tsp bicarbonate of soda | A knob of lard |

Place the barley meal, bicarbonate of soda and a pinch of salt in a bowl. Melt the butter and lard in half a cup of boiling water and add this to the meal, stirring well to a fairly stiff mixture. Then roll out gently until ½cm thick and bake on a fairly hot greased girdle, about 5–6 minutes for each side.

## Mull
## (Baking)

Flora Corbett has lived with her husband and children at Lochbuie in the south of Mull for nearly ten years. Her father-in-law owns the Lochbuie Estate and Flora and her husband Tim now help his father to run it. Flora bought the old post office at the beachside hamlet

*The Old Post Office at Lochbuie.*

of Lochbuie – a tiny building a stone's throw from Laggan beach – and decided to make it a shop, with an honesty box so that she was not tied to being there all the time. Her twins went to primary school in Craignure, some 35 minutes' drive away along single-track roads, and are now at secondary school in Tobermory, a good hour and a quarter away, so school buses must be met. The honesty-box system gave her more flexibility.

Flora sells local meat, including their own estate venison, Mull cheese and sausages made from pigs reared by Garth Reade at Isle of Mull Cheese. She also sells home-produced ready-meals, which she used to make herself but now has a producer make them up to her recipes, to free up a little time for her. These meals are hugely popular with the locals and also with holiday-makers in the many rented cottages all over Mull. Her most popular dishes are the venison lasagne and venison bourguignon, her lamb tagine and the pork and cider casserole made using island pork. The baking also goes down a storm, the favourites being brownies, flapjacks and Mag's fruit slice.

The Old Post Office has had a revamp since its original setting up as a tiny honesty-box shop – and in fact since my visit. It now has a small café and farm shop and is manned (womanned!) full-time, as it continues to be incredibly busy with locals and tourists.

Flora is chair of the local abattoir where Jeanette Cutlack works, using the offal for her delicious Mull haggis. Flora also helped set up the Mull and Iona Food Trail which includes the fabulous Calgary Arts Café in the north west at Calgary beach; the

*View from the Old Post Office.*

Tobermory Fish Company shop outside Tobermory; the Producers' markets at Dervaig, Craignure, Pennyghael and Tobermory; Duart Castle tearooms; and the Ninth Wave restaurant on the road to Iona. The criterion for places to be included in the Trail Guide are that a minimum of five local island ingredients must be used. At the Old Post Office at Lochbuie, Flora has local venison, meat, cheese, fish from the Tobermory Fish Company and salad bags from a Lochbuie resident who grows interesting salad leaves in her polytunnel.

From an honesty-box shop in a tiny shack, Flora has built a destination café and farm shop in one of the most stunning locations of any eating establishment. From the beach on the doorstep, you can see Colonsay, Islay and the tip of Jura on a clear day. Go there on such a clear, sunny day and you will think you are in the Caribbean; only with Highland cattle in the fields and sea eagles soaring around the cliffs of Mull.

# MAG'S FRUIT SLICE
*makes 12 slices*

*This recipe from Flora Corbett was given to her by her great friend Mag Macbeth, who is the Corbett family's general lifesaver and house-sitter extraordinaire. It goes down a treat at the Old Post Office at Lochbuie.*

| 350g self-raising flour | 2 tsp mixed spice |
| 285g demerara sugar and extra for sprinkling | 225g butter, melted |
| | 2 large eggs, beaten |
| 250g dried fruit (raisins, sultanas, glacé cherries) | |

Put everything in a bowl and mix well, then press into a buttered 23 x 33cm baking tray and sprinkle with a little more demerara sugar.

Bake at 180C/350F/Gas 4 for about 20 minutes until firm, then remove and allow to cool completely before cutting into bars.

# BO SIMMONS' GLUTEN-FREE APPLE CAKE

*serves 8*

*Since moving to Shetland nearly 30 years ago, Bo Simmons has become something of a culinary legend. With her husband Henry Anderton, they ran the fabulous Burrastow House which, during the 18 years they had the hotel, became famous throughout Scotland for its food. She trained as a chef and has always been passionate about good locally sourced food.*

*Now, as well as running a bed and breakfast house, she bakes for the wonderful Bonhoga Gallery in Weisdale in mainland Shetland. The Gallery is situated in Weisdale Mill, on land that had been cleared for large-scale sheep farming in the nineteenth century. It was a meal and barley mill from 1855 through until the early 1900s, then the Mill was used as a butchery and tannery before falling into dereliction in the middle of the twentieth century.*

*The building was renovated and opened as Bonhoga Gallery in 1994, and since then has been welcoming large numbers of visitors to see art and design exhibitions as well as visiting the café for Bo's delicious baking. Bonhoga means 'my spiritual home' in Shetland dialect.*

*This cake is a favourite of Bo and of the many gallery visitors. She also makes it with plums, apricots or pears, depending on the season. I like it also with brambles.*

200g caster sugar

100g gluten-free flour

100g ground almonds

3 medium free-range eggs

200ml vegetable oil

1tsp gluten-free baking powder

3 apples or 2 cooking apples, peeled and chopped quite small

*For the syrup:*

3 tbsp granulated or castor sugar

3 tbsp water

A pinch of cinnamon or a cinnamon stick

Mix all the cake ingredients except the apples together in a bowl. Pour the mixture into a round 20cm buttered and lined tin and scatter the apple on top. Put into a cold oven and turn on to 180C/350F/Gas 4 and bake for about 40–45 minutes, covering loosely with foil for the last 5 minutes to prevent burning, if necessary.

Whilst the cake is cooking, make the syrup. Place the sugar, water and cinnamon into a small pan and slowly bring to the boil, simmer for 1 minute and turn off. Once it is cool, remove the cinnamon stick if using.

When the cake is cooked, remove from the oven and pour over the syrup.

*West Burra, Shetland.*

# GAELIC COLLEGE
# MILLIONAIRE'S SHORTBREAD
*makes 20 pieces*

*Catriona McGillvary has been the cook at Café Blasta in Islay's Gaelic College in Bowmore for five years. As well as her coffee cake, scones, carrot cake and lemon coconut slice, it is her cloutie dumpling that all Islay residents rave about. She is known throughout the island for it, making it for island teas, ceilidhs and weddings. When I asked Catriona for the recipe, she said she could not give it to me as it was impossible to write down. She judged it as she mixed, a testament to a highly successful family recipe. Millionaire's Shortbread is possibly the next most popular of Catriona's bakes.*

For the base:

350g butter

350g plain flour

175g cornflour

100g caster sugar

For the toffee:

225g caster sugar

225g butter

4 tbsp golden syrup

1 x 397g tin condensed milk

For the topping:

250g best quality milk chocolate

First make the base. Melt the butter, add all the other ingredients and mix, then press into a 23 x 33cm lined tin and bake in a 160C/325F/Gas 3 oven for 30 minutes, remove and leave to cool.

Add all the toffee ingredients to a heavy-based saucepan and melt over a medium heat, then boil, stirring all the time until softball stage (test by dropping a little into cold water; it should form a soft ball), about 5–10 minutes. Pour this over the shortbread base.

When cool, top with melted chocolate, allowing this to cool before cutting into squares.

# ISLAY WHISKY CAKE

*serves 8–10*

*This delicious recipe is from Emma Goudie, who runs the exemplary Old Excise House B&B on the road out of Port Ellen on Islay towards the Laphroaig, Lagavulin and finally Ardbeg distilleries. Her husband Ron, a golf professional, is also a tour guide round Ardbeg distillery and so knows a thing or two about how good – but also how versatile – Islay whiskies are. Emma says this cake improves after a day or two.*

250g plain flour (Emma likes half wholemeal, half plain white)

2 level tsp baking powder

1 level tsp bicarbonate of soda

¼ tsp ground cloves

½ teaspoon ground cinnamon

225g light muscovado sugar

3 medium free-range eggs

125ml sunflower oil

75ml Islay whisky (Emma uses Ardbeg)

150g dates, chopped

100g walnuts, chopped

250g tinned pineapple, drained (reserve the juice) and chopped

*For the icing:*

100g icing sugar, sifted

2 tbsp Islay whisky

1 tbsp reserved pineapple juice

For the cake, butter and flour a 20cm round cake tin. Mix the flour, baking powder and bicarbonate of soda.

Place the spices and sugar in a large bowl and add the eggs. Beat with an electric beater for 3–4 minutes until light and fluffy, then add the oil and whisky, combining well. Gradually fold in the flour mixture, mixing until smooth, and add the dates, nuts and pineapple, mixing together. Tip the mixture into the prepared baking tin and bake in a preheated oven (180C/350F/Gas 4) for about 40 minutes or until the cake is firm to the touch. Remove to a wire rack to cool.

Make the icing by beating the icing sugar with the whisky and pineapple juice until you have a thin icing. Pour over the cake once it is cool.

*Opposite: Isle of Mull Cheese Soufflé.*

# 9
# Cheese

# Cheese
## (Isle of Mull)

When Chris and Jeff Reades moved to the island of Mull from Somerset in 1983 to farm dairy cows, they could hardly have envisaged that the small cheeses they began to make in a bucket would end up being sold in huge 22kg truckles and be so much in demand they can barely keep up.

But the Reade family continue to manage admirably to maintain high standards with their award-winning Isle of Mull cheese. Although they already knew about milk and dairy farming, they had to learn cheese-making from scratch in the dairy that came with Sgriob-ruadh Farm, near Tobermory, dating from the early 1800s. Their cheese is made to a traditional Cheddar-making recipe and so is defined as 'Cheddar-style', but differs, as according to Chris, 'it is a product of here'. The water and soil are different, as are the herbs the cows eat. The cows also eat draff (a by-product of ground-up malted barley from Tobermory's distillery) – all giving the cheese a unique character.

The milk from the Friesian-cross brown Swiss cows is unpasteurised and is made into a cheese that is matured for at least ten months in their cellars. The Reades would love to keep the cheese longer and mature it for more than a year, if only their long customer order list would allow! Not only do they make the huge cloth-bound truckles, but also baby truckles, 700g in weight, which are in particular demand over the Christmas period. Although a Cheddar cheese by definition, theirs is paler in colour and softer in texture and with a sharper flavour than those traditionally made in south west England. Chris describes the taste as tangy, spicy and creamy. It is also wonderfully smooth and infinitely moreish, excellent eaten 'neat' with bread or biscuits or, in true Scottish New Year tradition, served with shortbread. The Reade family also use it to bake cheesy oatcakes, cheese and onion tart and in all sorts of sauces and potato gratins.

Mull cheese is quite unique, with the entire family working to produce their wonderful cheese on the family farm. Most of their cows' milk goes to make 'Isle of Mull' and some also goes to make 'Hebridean Blue' which is an unpasteurised semi-soft blue.

Nowadays, Chris leaves the day-to-day running of the farm and dairy to her sons Brendan and Garth, and concentrates on managing the farm café. Locals and tourists alike flock here to be served simple, wholesome dishes, many made with the ingredients produced on the farm such as their own sausages; the pork is from their pigs which are fed on the whey produced during the cheese-making process.

Another son, Joe, runs the now famous Island Bakery, making excellent organic biscuits. He also used to bake bread and cakes in their Tobermory bakery and deli. This started in 1994 when he baked bread to sell in the van which his parents drove all over Mull (a 120-mile round trip), to sell their milk in their pre-cheese-making days. That worked for a while, but with the termination of the ferry service from Mull to Coll and Tiree, where they also supplied their bread, it was no longer financially viable, which is when they began baking their specialist organic biscuits. By 2007, the biscuit side of business had overtaken the deli, and so Joe and Dawn Reade made the difficult decision to sell their shop and concentrate on biscuits; they ended up building a new bakery which was completed in June 2012. Powered by local renewable energy – wind and water for electricity, and locally sourced firewood for heating the ovens – this has become a feel-good island success story.

And fortunately, among the places the Island Bakery biscuits are for sale are the Cal-Mac ferries. So on the crossing back from Mull to Oban, you can enjoy one of the Reades' delicious Lemon Melts, Oat Crumbles or Chocolate Limes with your cup of tea or coffee, as you look back over the water to the green pastures of the cows that provide milk for the island's famous cheese.

# ISLE OF MULL CHEESE OATCAKES
*makes 12*

*My recipe is based on Shelagh Reade's; Shelagh, married to Brendan Reade, makes her cheesy oatcakes for the farm shop on Mull during the busy summer months.*

*Do not even think about adding salt or other flavouring, as farmhouse cheese has enough superb taste all by itself. When not serving with the very obvious cheese and pickle – or soup or salad – I also like to serve them with slivers of Mull cheddar and thin slices of quince paste (membrillo).*

| | |
|---|---|
| 100g porridge oats | 75g butter, melted |
| 100g medium oatmeal | |
| 125g Isle of Mull (or other farmhouse) cheddar, finely grated | |

Mix the oats, oatmeal and cheese in a large bowl and slowly drizzle in the butter. Stir briefly with a wooden spoon to combine, adding just enough boiling water to form a firm paste, about 1½ tbsp. Then, using hands dipped in flour (or if you want them to be 100% wheat-free, dip in fine oatmeal), bring the dough together in your hands and pat out on a board. Just use the heels of your hands, not a rolling pin. Once the dough is reasonably thin, cut out 12 rounds, place these on a lightly buttered baking sheet and bake in a preheated oven (170C/325F/Gas 3) for 30–35 minutes or until they have crisped up and are golden brown. Cool on a wire rack.

# ISLE OF MULL CHEESE SOUFFLÉ
### serves 3–4

*If you have never made a soufflé before, let me assure you it's not only not difficult, it's astonishingly easy. If you can make a white sauce and whisk egg whites, you can make a soufflé. The quality of the cheese is of course paramount, so one as good as Mull Cheddar is to be recommended.*

| | |
|---|---|
| 50g butter | 4 large eggs, separated |
| 40g plain flour | 125g Isle of Mull Cheddar, grated |
| 300ml milk | 1 tsp Dijon mustard |

Melt the butter in a pan, stir in the flour and cook over a medium heat for a minute, stirring constantly. Remove from the heat and gradually stir in the milk, then exchange the wooden spoon for a whisk and cook over a medium heat until smooth and thickened, whisking constantly.

Beat in the egg yolks, one at a time, add the cheese and mustard, and season with salt and pepper.

Whisk the egg whites with a pinch of salt until stiff, and fold a couple of tablespoons gently into the cheese mixture. Then fold in the remainder.

Spoon this into a buttered 1.2 litre soufflé dish and bake in a preheated oven (190C/375F/Gas 5) for 35–40 minutes or until well risen and golden.

Serve at once with a salad and a good baguette.

# Tattie Scones with Cheese and Spinach

*makes 8*

*Eat these warm, with a thin smear of butter, whenever they are made; leftovers can be toasted the next day. They can also be made in advance; when you want them, loosely wrap in foil and reheat in a low oven.*

*Use a floury potato such as Maris Piper, King Edward or Pentland Dell.*

1 large potato (about 250g)

25g unsalted butter

50g plain flour

¼ tsp baking powder

40g grated mature cheese (such as Mull Cheddar)

100g baby spinach, cooked, chopped, well drained

Butter, to cook

Peel the potato, cut into chunks and cook in boiling water until tender; drain well. Using a potato masher, mash the potato with the butter.

Sift the flour, ½ tsp of salt and the baking powder into a bowl. While the mash is still warm, stir into the flour and combine well with the cheese and spinach. Using lightly floured hands, gently shape this mixture into two balls and turn onto a lightly floured surface. With a rolling pin, roll out very gently to form two circles about 5mm thick. Cut each circle into quarters. Prick all over with a fork.

Heat the girdle (or heavy frying pan) to medium-hot, smear over a little butter, and once it is hot, transfer four scones to it with a large spatula or fish slice. Cook for about 3–4 minutes each side, until golden brown. Transfer to a wire rack to cool briefly, before spreading with a little butter and eating warm.

# Cullen Skink with Isle of Mull Cheddar Crouton

*serves 4*

*This recipe is based on one Sally Swinbanks from Tobermory Fish Company gave me. The cheesy crunch of the toasted crouton is both unexpected and delicious.*

25g butter

1 large leek, trimmed and sliced finely

1 large onion, peeled and chopped finely

1 large potato, peeled and diced

1 litre chicken or vegetable stock

200ml double cream

2 large fillets of smoked haddock, chopped into chunks

2 slices of sourdough bread

125g Isle of Mull Cheddar, grated

Melt the butter, add the leeks and onions, and when they are soft, add the chopped potatoes and stir. Put in the stock and seasoning and simmer on a low heat for 15 minutes.

When the potatoes are cooked, add the double cream and simmer for a further couple of minutes, then add the smoked haddock, cook for 2 minutes and turn off the heat.

Toast your sourdough and chop each slice in half. Top with Isle of Mull Cheddar and put under the grill until the cheese is bubbling and melted. Meanwhile, check the seasoning of the soup, reheat a little if necessary, ladle into warm bowls and top with the cheesy crouton and black pepper.

## Westray Wife Cheese
### (Westray)

Nina and Jason Wilson moved into their farm on the Orkney island of Westray in 2012 and began the long process, firstly of adapting a former beef farm into a dairy, then starting the conversion to full organic status. Jason spent a year studying cheese-making, having worked on farms all over the UK as a fruit and vegetable picker and ending up as farm manager. He completed his cheese-making training with two weeks at Locharthur dairy, where Barry Graham and his team make his award-winning artisan cheeses. Nina and Jason were fortunate to meet many cheese-makers on their travels and get inspiration and advice for the types of cheeses they hoped to make one day. Their favourites were Alpine cheese (they liked the sweet nutty flavour and the melting quality) and, inspired by these cheese-making greats, they soon began to make their own. Theirs are bacteria-ripened (rather than the more usual mould-ripening in the UK) in the continental style.

Eventually, having been approved by environmental agencies, they were up and running as a dairy, producing cheese and yoghurt, by the autumn of 2015. They have a herd of 20 Ayrshire cows that graze on certified organic grassland on the northern coast of Westray, near the ruined sixteenth-century Noltland Castle. The varied diet of the cows – there are some 40 different types of grasses from clovers to parsley as grazing – helps give a unique flavour to both the milk and the cheese. All the milk they use for the cheese is their own and fully organic, although they have not certified the creamery and its products. It seems obvious to say that the Wilsons use only milk from their own herd of Ayrshires to produce their cheese. But in fact many dairies are able to buy in milk to supplement their own. The Wilsons do not sell their milk locally, even though it is now pasteurised by a method called 'batch pasteurisation', which is a far more gentle means of pasteurising milk than the standard way, as it is done at a lower temperature than usual and for a longer time. As Jason tells me, 'We are trying to be as gentle and as respectful to the milk as possible.'

Jason and Nina do most of the work at the dairy, and so must both milk the cows and make the cheese themselves, day after day. When I asked when they last had a holiday, Jason laughed. 'It's not something that's been possible, as there's always something to do and we see it as a way of life. We're fulfilled being dairy farmers and cheese-makers, though needless to say it's probably not for everyone!'

It's also relentlessly hard work, but a process which is always fascinating with so many variations depending on the often harsh climate. When pushed on how long the 4kg cheeses mature before being ready for sale, Jason tells me a winter cheese could be ready at two months and will taste fresher and sweeter; a summer one could take four to five months to mature and would be stronger flavoured as the conditions are milder.

Once the cheeses are shaped into rounds, the rinds are washed in a salty brine, which Nina tells me reminds her of the salty waves lapping up on the shore down from the farm. Westray is an island one and a half hours by ferry to the north-west of mainland Orkney, north of Rousay and west of Papa Westray. It has a population of nearly 600. The Wilsons never sell a whole round of Westray Wife as they always like to cut and taste each one before selling.

The cheese is called Westray Wife after a small neolithic figurine, about 5,000 years old, found in an archaeological dig on the Links of Noltland, beside their farm, in 2009. Also known as the Orkney Venus and locally as the Westray Wifie, it is the earliest human carving to be found in Scotland and is the first representation of a human face in Europe. As for the taste of this wonderfully named cheese, it has been described as earthy and nutty, with a farmyard characteristic. I love its rich grassy taste and also its texture which is yielding yet firm: it is defined as a semi-hard cheese. It also has a good buttery taste from the creamy rich milk. It is not only delicious eaten with good bread or oatcakes; the Wilsons like to use it in cauliflower cheese, then convert any leftovers into soup. Local Orkney hotels use it in a tartlet with caramelised red onions or a soufflé with apple and walnut.

The Wilsons also make two cheeses sold locally on Orkney – Noltland Castle and Cannonball (the latter a cloth-hung cheese in the style of mozzarella or feta).

The Wilsons of Westray have managed, over only some three years of hard work and dedication, to produce cheeses that are now sold throughout the country in the best cheesemongers; they are also winning numerous awards. Westray Wife has become a great favourite of mine too and I love to eat it as it is, at room temperature (never straight from the fridge), with good bread – or cooked in dishes such as macaroni cheese or cheese on toast, or as wonderful bite-size canapés, Cheese and Chilli Puffs.

# CHEESE AND CHILLI PUFFS
## makes 24–30

*These are the easiest cheesy canapés you will ever make and are based on my friend Isabelle's recipe – so quick to rustle up. Yet when you serve them with drinks, there will always be someone asking for the recipe. As an alternative to the chilli flavour, you can ring the changes by adding a handful of chopped basil leaves in place of the chilli.*

1 large free-range egg

125ml milk

150g plain flour, sifted

2 level tsp baking powder

200g grated cheese (I like to
use Westray Wife or Isle of
Mull Cheddar)

1 red chilli, seeds removed,
finely chopped (or 6 large
basil leaves, chopped)

Beat the egg into the milk. Mix together the flour, baking powder, cheese and a pinch of salt, then add the chilli (or basil).

Place large teaspoons of the mixture on a cold buttered baking tray, and bake in a preheated oven (200C/400F/Gas 6) for 10–12 minutes, until puffed up and golden brown. Eat warm.

*Cheese and Chilli Puffs.*

# Isle of Lewis Cheese Company
## (Lewis)

When Dave and Jane Eastwood left the Midlands in 2005 and bought a croft some 15 minutes north of Stornoway on the island of Lewis, their intention was to run a B&B. They had some other plans as well. Jane established a croft garden to supply both vegetables and their own free-range eggs to guests. She also provides therapy, as she is trained in reflexology and reiki. Dave, as well as running the croft, does some blacksmithing; he was a blacksmith when they lived in the Midlands. The B&B guests have not only delicious breakfasts, but occasionally Dave and Jane provide them with dinner using as much of their own produce as possible.

Over their early years on the croft, they began teaching themselves how to make cheese and eventually Dave did a cheese-making course at West Highland Dairy. The local Environmental Health Board helped them set up their own dairy as this was a unique business enterprise, reviving the art of island cheese-making on Lewis. Crowdie is of course the only cheese that is truly Hebridean; and that became a best-seller.

The Eastwoods have four goats – two British Toggenburg and two cross. Their milk is available after kidding for some ten months, from February until Christmas. They tried hand-feeding the kids after a week, but this was such a lot of extra work, they now leave the kids on the nannies during the day, then milk the morning milk for themselves. Win, win! – as they are sharing the milk with the kids.

The goat's cheeses are made from the end of March but now are not available for sale. They continue to make the cheeses – however, sadly, as is too often the case with artisan cheesemakers, it became unsustainable. So now they make the wonderful cheeses for themselves, for use in their B&B and to give as gifts to friends. Lucky friends! Their range included a soft goat's cheese called Vatisker; a hard goat's cheese called White Raven and a washed curd cheese called Breibhig Tom, matured for three to five months. They now make an unpasteurised Tom and enjoy it in quiches or in a croque monsieur on sourdough bread. Local chefs have used the White Raven grated over local black pudding and grilled until golden. I like to use the Tom in a simple omelette, using local Hebridean eggs.

# ISLE OF LEWIS CHEESE OMELETTE

*serves 2*

*I made this in our rented house on Scalpay using fabulous eggs from Anna's Honesty Box along the road. The same eggs are used in George Lavery's kitchen at the Scalpay bistro. I used the Eastwoods' Isle of Lewis Breibhig Tom cheese, but any other washed curd, hard, easy-melting goat's cheese will do.*

*I like to eat this with some good bread and a simple tomato salad, dressed with a light vinaigrette.*

6 large free-range eggs

25g butter

125g Isle of Lewis Breibhig Tom, sliced (or easy-melting goat's cheese)

Whisk the eggs gently and season with salt and pepper. Melt the butter in a frying pan, put in the eggs and leave to set around the edges before tipping the pan and allowing the liquid eggs to flow around. Once nearly set but still very wobbly, add the cheese to one side, carefully flip the other half of omelette over the top and continue to cook for a further minute or two, till the outsides are set and the insides are still soft and the cheese molten.

Eat at once with bread and a tomato salad.

*Anna's honesty box, Scalpay.*

# CROWDIE AND SMOKED FISH PATÉ

*serves 4–6*

*I used to make this with Isle of Lewis Cheese Company's crowdie cheese, but since, sadly, they no longer make it, I use other traditionally made crowdie. Crowdie is good in fish patés, with its unique smooth yet firm texture, and with a sharp lemony taste. Otherwise you can use ricotta (although it is not as low-fat as crowdie, which has only 4.5g of fat per 100g) and though the taste is still good the overall texture will be softer.*

*Any island hot-smoked salmon or trout is suitable for this simple, quick recipe. I like to use lovage in it but you can also use chives or parsley. Serve with thick oatcakes or warm bannocks.*

200g hot-smoked salmon or trout, skin removed, flesh flaked

150g crowdie cheese

2 tbsp lovage leaves

Juice of 1½ lemons

Whizz everything together in a blender or food processor. Taste and add pepper as necessary (you should not need any salt).

Chill before serving.

*Opposite: Colonsay Honey Ice-cream.*

# Honey and Gin

# Honey
## (Colonsay)

When you attend a book festival as an author, you are invariably given a goody bag, something to look forward to with anticipation. Sometimes you find a book, a pen, a scarf or even some whisky. But without doubt, one of the most welcome gifts I have received as an author was at the Colonsay Book Festival in 2017. There in my bedroom at the Colonsay Hotel was a jar of the island's honey. What a nice touch, I agreed with my fellow authors, and thought nothing more of it until the following morning when the same honey appeared on the breakfast table. The taste was and is exquisite, unlike any other honeys I have tasted. Nuanced and floral, the texture is rich, creamy and unctuous. I was hooked over breakfast and could not wait to find out more about this honey's provenance.

Andrew Abrahams has been producing Isle of Colonsay Wildflower Honey for some four decades, a labour of love that he fits in between his many other jobs, including that of oyster farmer. Andrew lives at the Strand, right at the south end of Colonsay opposite the small tidal island of Oronsay and has beehives – some 50 to 60 – all over both islands. His bees are a strain of the native black bee, whose hardiness means they are able to harvest on cool, sunless days and even in a strong wind.

When I asked Andrew about the distinctive, complex flavour of his honey, he summed it up perfectly by telling me it is 'the essence of all the flowers on Colonsay'. There is a lot of heather in it – and unusually there is both ling and bell heather. Most heathers in Scotland grow on moorland; on the island, however, they also grow on rocks and this gives a different flavour to the honey. There are also wild thyme, clover, sea pinks, hawthorn and many more flowers growing on the sandy machair and on the moors of Colonsay.

The honey is harvested once a year, usually in September, and then comes the process of extracting the honey from the wooden frames of honeycomb. Honey is extracted by centrifrugal force, usually radially. However, given the high proportion of heather, those honeys with the specific consistency that Andrew's have are extracted tangentially instead. They are then potted into jars and labelled with a picture of the Celtic cross representing Oronsay's fourteenth-century priory.

When asked how he likes to eat it and if he has any particularly recipe using honey he would like to share, Andrew insists you mustn't mess about with it. Apart from serving it with ice-cream where it is simple enough to retain the pure honey flavour, he says why eat it with anything other than on a simple piece of bread or toast. In times past on the

Scottish islands, honey was eaten with bannocks made of beremeal or oats (and sometimes rye) and it was used as a sweetener in that harvest-time pudding, Cranachan, made from hedgerow brambles, crowdie and toasted oats. There are also some old recipes that predate the arrival of sugar to Scotland, in rich game dishes such as hare with honey and claret. Personally, I like to use it in simple recipes, but best of all, with honey as delicious as Andrew's Colonsay honey, I also like to eat it neat, from a spoon, straight out of the jar. Nectar.

# COLONSAY HONEY ICE-CREAM
*serves 6–8*

*I had finished the jar of honey I brought back from the Colonsay Book Festival with indecent haste on my return to Edinburgh, but my agent Jenny managed to buy the last two jars in the village shop on Colonsay when she was there. And with this, I made this exquisite ice-cream. Because the recipe is so simple, the true, floral, elusive taste of island honey takes centre stage.*

| | |
|---|---|
| 600ml double cream | 1 397g tin of condensed milk |
| 4 heaped tbsp Colonsay honey | Strawberries/raspberries and perhaps some shortbread, to serve |
| ¼ tsp of sea salt | |

Pour the cream into a bowl and whisk gently (at low speed if using an electric mixer) for a couple of minutes, then increase to a medium speed (or use a heavier hand whisk!) until you can see it start to thicken.

Now add the honey, one spoon at a time, whisking after each spoonful. Add the salt and continue to whisk until you have soft peaks, then pour in the condensed milk. Using a large metal spoon, combine gently until thoroughly combined. It should be light and thick. Pour this mixture into a freezer container, seal tightly and pop in the freezer for several hours (at least 6 hours) or overnight. Let it wait at room temperature for a couple of minutes before serving, perhaps with some shortbread and berries: both strawberries and raspberries go well with honey.

# HONEY CHEESECAKE ICE-CREAM

*serves 6*

*This is a luscious ice-cream that has overtones of cheesecake, as it is cream cheese based, with only a little double cream. The quality and flavour of the honey is crucial to the finished ice-cream; runny honey is best, but if your favourite honey is thick, then warm slightly so it becomes a little liquid and add to the food processor to blend well. Serve with some crumbled digestive biscuits to simulate a cheesecake base.*

| | |
|---|---|
| 450g cream cheese | 1 tsp vanilla bean paste |
| 150g honey (I like Colonsay or Islay) | 300ml double cream |
| 2 tsp liquid glucose | 2–3 digestive biscuits, crushed |

Place the cream cheese in a food processor and whizz until smooth, add the honey, glucose and vanilla and combine again. Then, with the machine running, add the cream through the feeder tube. Once this is well combined, scrape down the sides and blend again.

Now it is thoroughly combined, tip into a freezer box, cover tightly and freeze for at least 3 hours, until it is starting to freeze at the sides. Tip back into the food processor, whizz briefly and return to the box. Cover again and freeze until firm. Remove from the freezer some 20 minutes or so before you are ready to eat and serve in scoops, dusted with some biscuit crumbs.

# Honey
## (Scalpay)

Chris Loye is a hugely talented young chef who, after training in Glasgow, worked in Ayrshire before setting out on his travels: to India, Thailand and Colombia and ending up in Australia, where, with his partner Nicola, he worked and picked up cooking tips from the great chefs there. His first job as head chef was on Thursday Island to the north of the Great Barrier Reef. After living the dream there, he felt it was time to return home to Scotland. There he worked with an agency which among other things catered on set for the *Outlander* series. He ended up in Harris in 2016 on seasonal cooking jobs; and that was when they decided to stay. They bought a house near the beach at Niseaboist on West Harris and started catering for guests on nearby self-accommodation holidays. After this they began to set up pop-up restaurants, both in their house, where they can seat up to 14, and in venues all over the island.

Nicola now also makes the most exquisite chocolates which are on sale all over Harris and also feature as part of the six-course menu he provides for guests. They travelled to Central America to learn more about chocolate, from the cocoa pods on the tree to making it in true artisan style. Her flavours include raspberry with dark chocolate, Harris gin with white chocolate and single flavoured Scalpay honey. Chris gets his honey from a

*Luskentyre, Harris.*

Scalpay local called Roddy who keeps native Hebridean black bees. He has five hives and a garden full of all sorts of different flowers and shrubs, which give the honey a wonderfully sweet and deep flavour. Chris also uses his honey in a Scalpay honey posset which is one of the favourites on his menu. This might follow a starter of goat's cheese soufflé then scallops and venison loin with butternut squash puree and red cabbage. Canapés might be quail Scotch eggs wrapped in Stornoway black pudding, using eggs from quails farmed on the nearby Borve estate. He gets most of his vegetables from a grower near the beautiful Luskentyre Beach: carrots, kail, leeks, beetroot, beans, tomatoes and onions. As much as possible, he cooks with local produce. The chocolate, admittedly, has to be imported, but the ingredients he combines them with are local. This is a very fine chef who is going places – he has plans to have his own restaurant premises soon and also to set up chocolate-making classes with Nicola – but, luckily for the inhabitants of Harris, he is staying put.

# SCALPAY HONEY POSSET
*serves 6*

*I have reduced the quantities in this divine yet easy recipe from Chris, who likes to serve it with shortbread and berries or seasonal fruit. He strains the mixture through a fine sieve, but I have eliminated this for the home cook.*
*Colonsay honey is also good in this; indeed use any good honey with a pleasantly floral taste.*

500ml double cream

100g Scalpay honey (or other good quality honey)

40ml lemon juice (juice of approx. 2 lemons)

Heat the cream and honey in a pan over a medium heat, stirring to ensure all the honey is dissolved. Once it has come to the boil, reduce the heat to a gentle boil for a further 3 minutes, stirring constantly. Remove from the heat, add the lemon juice and stir well for 30 seconds to ensure it is thoroughly mixed.

Pour into ramekins or espresso cups, then gently tap the base on your working surface to remove any air bubbles trapped on the surface. Place in the refrigerator for at least 2 to 3 hours to ensure the possets are set.

Serve with shortbread and berries.

# Gin
## (Harris)

Harris distillery is called The Social Distillery for several reasons.

The businessman Anderson Bakewell had had connections with the island of Harris for some years before he decided to set up a project that would help support the falling population by providing employment; he also wanted to somehow 'bottle the island'. And the means he chose was to set up the Isle of Harris Distillers Ltd, whose aim was to enrich the island and to have the future benefit of Harris at its heart. The distillery opened in October 2015, and since the whisky industry is a long-term investment, with the whisky requiring years to mature, it was decided that gin would be made alongside it. The whisky is called The Hearach, the local name for a Harris dweller.

With the help of private and public sector investment, this fabulous Harris distillery began distilling its now world-famous gin which continues to be successful because, according to commercial manager Shona Macleod, it is and has always been, firstly about the taste of the spirit, then also about the story behind it and the packaging. The spirit, like other island gins, is unique because of its botanicals. Sea kelp is the island ingredient that gives it such a glorious dry maritime note. The sea kelp was suggested to be used as one of the botanicals by an ethnobotanist, who saw it not only as a sustainable botanical but also as an embodiment of Harris, which is surrounded by shores rich in seaweed.

The story of Harris gin is that, from a small operation at the start, they now employ nearly 30 people and the Distillery café and shop are so popular, they have visitors from far and wide just to buy a bottle of gin in the shop or to eat one of Irene's famous scones in the café. The café only serves soups, light salads and baking as it does not want to provide competition for other island cafés; again, this is all about the community spirit behind the distillery.

And as for the packaging, very few bottles can claim to be quite as iconic as those of Harris gin. Everywhere you travel around the Outer Hebrides, the empty bottles are being used as water bottles or table lamps. The 'upcycling' of the bottles is part of the sustainability story. And on the base, etched into the glass, is 'Esse Quam Videri' – 'To be rather than to seem'. The people from the company behind the design spent some time on Harris, drams in hand, on the beach at sunset, before coming up with the cool logo and bottle design which speaks so much of the island.

*Isle of Harris Gin.*

So now, given its huge popularity, instead of creating gin about once a week as predicted at the start, it is being made at least three times a week, such is the demand.

There is only one gin still which is called The Dottach after a local woman. The botanicals are macerated for some 24 hours to ensure a full flavour. And as for the resulting spirit? The tasting notes suggest a distinctive, dry, flinty taste. It is recommended to be drunk either on the rocks, perhaps with extra sugar kelp added, or with a wedge of pink grapefruit and tonic water. It is also versatile and used in many recipes, especially with seafood and pickled vegetables, as the maritime overtones of these match the gin perfectly. Elegant and eminently quaffable, Harris gin not only has a feel-good island story, it tastes divine.

# SMOKED MACKEREL, BABY POTATO, CRISPY BACON SALAD WITH ISLE OF HARRIS GIN-INFUSED CAPER DRESSING

*serves 4*

*This recipe is from Kate Macdougall, who runs the Harris Gin Distillery canteen. Soaking the capers in the gin makes such a difference to the overall taste. You have to try it to believe it!*

1 medium onion, peeled and sliced

3 tbsp white wine vinegar

6 rashers of smoked bacon

4 smoked mackerel fillets

500g baby potatoes, boiled for about 15 mins until tender

*For the dressing and serving:*

2 tsp Dijon mustard

6 tbsp olive oil

A splash of lemon juice

4 sprigs of fresh dill, roughly chopped

1 heaped tsp capers, soaked in Isle of Harris Gin (enough to cover) for 30 minutes

Place the onion in a bowl. Cover with the vinegar for 10 minutes – this will remove the onion's harshness and soften it slightly. Place the bacon on a tray and grill until crispy, then roughly chop into chunky pieces.

For the dressing, simply put Dijon mustard in a bowl, add the vinegar the onions have soaked in, and whisk together, adding the olive oil a little at the time until it thickens. Season with black pepper and a splash of lemon juice to taste. Drain the potatoes and add them to the dressing while still warm. Divide and pile the potatoes on four plates. Add the onions, capers, crispy bacon, dill and the smoked mackerel that has been flaked in chunks over the potatoes and serve.

# HARRIS GIN MAYO
*makes enough for 4*

*Adding Harris Gin to mayonnaise or tartare sauce that you serve with fish is wonderful, as the sea kelp notes come through even though you are not adding much. So instead of squeezing in some lemon juice at the end of the mayonnaise-making, I stir in some gin.*

| | |
|---|---|
| I large free-range egg yolk | Approx. 100ml mild olive oil |
| I tsp Dijon mustard | ½-1 tbsp Harris Gin |

Whisk together the yolk and mustard, add some salt, then, drop by drop at first, add the oil, whisking all the time. Soon you can add the oil in a slow drizzle, but do not glug it in! Once it is thick and creamy, add a half tablespoon of gin and taste. Add more salt and pepper if you need, and a splash more gin if the flavour is not coming through – it should be a background hint, not an alcoholic blast!

Serve with fish and chips.

## Lussa Gin
## (Jura)

In 2016, three local Jura women – Claire Fletcher, Georgina Kitching and Alicia MacInnes – made their first batch of Lussa Gin in Jim, the original still. As the popularity of their gin spread and Jim became too small, the increased production now required happens in Hamish, a copper still with a capacity of 200 litres. But they use exactly the same method, by filling the still with a mixture of spring water and ethanol and adding the robust botanicals; the more tender ones are added to the mix in a copper pot at the top of the still.

They use fifteen botanicals from all over the island, including lemon thyme, juniper, wild watermint, bog myrtle, ground elder, rose hips, sea lettuce, lime flowers and rose petals. From the start of Lussa Gin, with a few bottles produced in the stables of Claire Fletcher's family home, it is now on a much larger scale, but still made by hand by three Jura women, who are passionate about putting a taste of Jura into bars and kitchens across the land.

*Lussa Gin.*

They organised a tasting of their gin in the one and only pub on Jura, the fabulous bar of the Jura Hotel, with the purpose of deciding which tonic water goes best with their gin. None of your fancy schmancy tonic waters for Lussa; the overall winner was Britvic Tonic. And indeed perhaps a plain tonic water brings out better the wonderful flavour and floral nose from the fragrant rose petals, elderflower and honeysuckle.

When I asked them how they like to use their Lussa Gin, Claire said she likes to use it in a venison pie; Georgina likes it in a lemon gin drizzle cake; and Alicia simply likes to drink it – neat. There is surely no better testament to how good this island gin is.

Georgina and Claire's teenage children, James and Pete Kitching and Molly, Scarlet, Kitty and Tabitha Fletcher, are becoming as enterprising as their mothers. They run Tea on the Beach on beautiful Inverlussa beach, just a mile down the road from the distillery. Throughout the summer months, they bake three delicious cakes and provide tea and coffee on the beach with thermoses of hot water and fresh milk. When I was there the bakes were brownies, coffee cake and the moistest, most delicious lemon drizzle cake. There is an honesty box there for people to pay for such an excellent and unexpected treat. Who would expect both award-winning gin and superb cakes to come from a tiny hamlet on the east of Jura?

# Lussa Gin Cured Salmon

*serves many*

*This is Lizzie Massie's wonderful recipe for cured salmon, using her sister-in-law's Jura gin.*

8 tbsp Lussa Gin

70g caster sugar

50g sea salt

A handful of chopped dill

I tsp fennel seeds.

2 x 750g salmon fillets, skin on.

To serve:

Garden herb and lemon scones (dainty savoury scones with the addition of finely chopped herbs and lemon zest)

Pea shoot salad (pea shoots with a light vinaigrette)

Mix together the gin, sugar and salt, and add the chopped herbs and spices and a good twist of black pepper.

Spread the mixture over both the salmon fillets, and sandwich the fillets together. Wrap in clingfilm, place on a plate and weigh down with something heavy. Leave in the fridge for 1 to 3 days. Serve thinly sliced with the scones and a pea shoot salad.

*Inverlussa, Jura.*

# JURA VENISON GIN PIE

*serves 6*

*This is Claire Fletcher's recipe using Lussa Gin and local Jura venison.*

50g butter

1 large onion, thinly sliced

100g diced pancetta or bacon

250ml Lussa Gin

1 heaped tbsp plain flour

1kg diced venison (large chunks, preferably shoulder or leg, and definitely red deer)

1 tsp wholegrain mustard

2 large carrots, peeled and diced

1 tbsp soft brown sugar

1 tbsp rowan jelly (or redcurrant if you can't find rowan)

250ml beef stock

1 sprig of fresh thyme

1 tbsp Worcester sauce

1 block of the best puff pastry you can buy

1 egg and milk for pastry

Preheat the oven to 150C/300F/Gas 2.

Melt the butter in the casserole dish on the hob and add the sliced onion and pancetta. Once the onions are soft and transparent, which always takes longer than you think, increase the heat and add the gin. It needs to bubble to take out the alcohol, but after a minute or two turn the heat back down and add the flour, then turn off the heat.

If you brown the venison, Claire says, it tightens up which makes it tough, so add the venison now to the dish along with all the other ingredients and plenty of ground black pepper; but do not yet add salt (which you'll add at the end of cooking, as again it can make the meat tough).

Put the lid on the casserole dish and cook gently and slowly for a couple of hours. Check it and stir it now and then, and take the lid off for the last half hour. Once it's tender, take it out of the oven, add salt to taste and set aside.

Increase the temperature of the oven to 190C/375F/Gas 5.

Roll out the pastry thickly and cut around the pie dish with a 1cm overhang and cut out a stag shape.

Transfer the contents of the casserole to the pie dish and drape the pastry over it, adding the stag. Crimp the edges of the pastry with a fork leaving a bit of an overhang as it will shrink back. Beat an egg with a tablespoon of milk and brush over the pastry. Make a couple of holes with the tip of a knife to let the air out and bake in a hot oven for about 40 minutes until the pastry is golden brown.

Serve with mashed potato and greens.

*Young stag on Jura.*

# THE JURA HOTEL'S GIN AND TONIC SORBET

*serves 8*

*When you hear that the Jura Hotel is the only hotel on the island, you wonder if it's any good, since there is no competition. Well, as it turns out, it most certainly is. The warmth of the welcome in both hotel and the snug lively pub adjoining it, are memorable. And in the restaurant the chef, Stuart Russell, is providing excellent food, most of which uses local ingredients. He serve s up Jura venison haunch steaks in a delicious bramble and red wine sauce, and also uses langoustines, lobster, squat lobsters and octopus, landed daily by a local fisherman. Their Lussa Gin sorbet is divine.*

800ml caster sugar

800ml water

800ml tonic water

180ml Lussa Gin

Grated zest and juice of 2 lemons

Grated zest and juice of 2 limes

Boil the water and sugar until the sugar has dissolved, turn up the heat and boil for 3 to 4 minutes, without stirring, until you have a stock syrup.

Once this has thoroughly cooled, add the tonic water and then the gin, lemon and lime. Now churn in an ice-cream machine until solid. Remove from the freezer for 5 minutes or so to come to room temperature before serving.

# Gin
## (Skye)

Thomas and Alistair Wilson set up the Isle of Skye Distillery, producing Misty Isle Gin, in early February 2017, to great acclaim. All their gin is made locally in Portree, using the crystal-clear spring waters from the Storr Loch, just over a mile or so from the distillery. They first launched as Isle of Skye gin and are the first stills producing gin on Skye!

There are eleven botanicals used in Misty Isle: juniper, coriander, black cubeb, grains of paradise, angelica root, cassia bark, liquorice root, lemon, lemon verbena and orris root; and the eleventh is a secret island ingredient that only the two brothers know. All Alistair would tell me when I tried to push him on the elusive botanical, is that it is foraged on Skye and dried to a crisp, then mixed in with the orris root. The gin is distilled in the three 100-litre traditional copper pot stills, then the baskets of botanicals are introduced to add the unique flavour profile.

*Misty Isle Gin.*

After their opening in 2017, they produced over 14,000 bottles within a year and can scarcely keep up with demand. They now sell from their own shop in Portree and also online all over the UK. Since there are just the two of them running the distillery and sales, it is relentless work; but satisfying to know their gins are so well loved.

Their second gin, Tommy's Gin (named after their late father) is flavoured with juniper, poppy seeds, orange peel, blaeberries, orange – and again, other botanicals which are secret.

Both gins are used by local chefs. Some marinate their seafood in it, some make fudge or use it in a cranachan instead of whisky. It is also used in cranberry jelly with venison, in lemon sorbet and in cheesecakes.

# ISLE OF SKYE GIN TABLET
*makes about 30 pieces*

*This is based on the Wilson brothers' mother Kirsty's famous tablet recipe, handed down from the brothers' great-great-grandmother. Here it is enlivened by a good splash of their famous gin. I think the spicy (almost cinnamon-like) flavour of Misty Isle gin brings out the richness of this delicious traditional recipe.*

125g salted butter

1kg granulated sugar

300ml semi-skimmed milk

1 x 397g tin of condensed milk

1 tsp vanilla extract

75ml Misty Isle Gin

Gently melt the butter, sugar and milk in a pan. Remove from the heat and stir in the condensed milk. Bring the mixture back to the boil for 10 minutes, stirring constantly. Then add the vanilla and continue to heat for a further 10 minutes, now beating constantly with the wooden spoon.

Add the gin, then remove from the heat and continue to beat, by hand for 8 to 10 minutes or with an electric beater for 4 to 5 minutes, until smooth. Pour at once into a greased Swiss-roll tin (23 x 33cm). Cut into pieces using a hot knife.

# Gin
## (Islay)

Bruichladdich Distillery, with its name in aqua-blue colours bold against the whitewashed stone walls, is a striking building dating from 1881 on the shores of Lochindaal, Islay. As well as the hundreds of daily visitors keen to taste the well-known whisky, the distillery also runs tours showcasing the award-winning gin called The Botanist, created first at Bruichladdich in 2010.

The concept of its creators was to make a gin that embodied the island, and so foraging experts combed the island of Islay to find all the possible botanicals available. From 33 Islay botanicals, they selected 22 to combine in a perfect balance of flavours to make their stunning gin. These include apple mint, chamomile, downy birch, gorse, sweet cicely, tansy, wild thyme, heather and of course juniper. And because foraging is so crucial to the production of the gin, the distillery holds local foraging tours for both locals and specialist chefs; they also offer superb Botanist dinners for the visiting chefs.

Chef Craig Grozier of Glasgow's Fallachan private dining, who is on Islay cooking with The Botanist for two weeks a month over the summer months, is the force behind these incredible Botanist gin dinners. His menus include Islay langoustine with pine, rose and onion; saltmarsh lamb with dulse and sea succulents; and tart of sea buckthorn with buckwheat koji. This is fine dining as befits a truly elegant gin. Having worked as a chef in high-end restaurants all over the world, Craig uses his expertise – plus his knowledge of Islay's foraging potential – to create unique dishes, many of which incorporate The Botanist gin. Another of his favourites is cured herring with gin.

Scotland's only full-time foraging tutor, Mark Williams, leads foraging tours all over Islay, revealing, to both locals and visiting chefs, what the island has on offer. Locals in particular are amazed at the abundance of leaves and herbs literally at their feet. When I visited the distillery, there was a group of bartenders from all over the world participating in a 'wild cocktail' competition, using The Botanist gin and locally foraged botanics. The results were extraordinary – some of cocktails made using The Botanist contain gorse syrup, lemon balm, wild berries, hawthorn, sour dock and rose petals. The Botanist is not only very much an island gin, it is a spirit of our time.

# THE BOTANIST CHEESECAKE
### *serves 10*

*This wonderful cheesecake is made by Islay cook Kelsey Leslie using The Botanist gin. I like to serve it with raspberries or strawberries.*

| | |
|---|---|
| ½ x 397g tin of condensed milk | 2–3 tbsp lemon curd, for topping |
| 200g cream cheese | For the base: |
| 500ml double cream, lightly whipped | 225g digestives or ginger nuts, crushed |
| 100ml Botanist gin plus extra for topping | 100g butter, melted |

For the base, combine the biscuits and butter and press into a buttered 23cm deep baking tin (with removable base). Chill.

For the filling, fold the condensed milk and cream cheese into the whipped cream, then gradually add the gin and combine, using a light whisking action. Once this mixture is smooth, spoon over the base and chill. To serve, melt the lemon curd with a splash of gin until just runny (do not overheat) and drizzle this over the top,

*The Botanist Cheesecake.*

# GIN AND TONIC CAKE

*serves 8*

*When I was at the Colonsay Book Festival, we authors had lunch and tea in the community hall with the audience on both Saturday and Sunday. Delicious home-made soup was served at lunch, but it was the home-baking at tea time that blew me away. Grace Johnston was in charge of all the cakes and scones; a keen baker and hospitality manager by profession, she also runs island supper clubs regularly. Her husband Keir runs the island's only shop, so the Johnstons are well known by every single one of the 125 islanders. And they all know her baking skills.*

*Among her many delicious bakes that weekend, it was her Gin and Tonic Cake that I loved most. Grace likes to use the island brewery's Wild Island Gin but the second gin made on the island – Colonsay Gin – is also more than acceptable.*

*Grace likes to make two separate round cakes, sandwich them together with lemon curd and drizzle the topping over once cold. I prefer a square cake and I always put the topping on the minute the cake is out of the oven. Grace also uses margarine for a better rise; I prefer, always, the flavour of butter.*

| | |
|---|---|
| 225g unsalted butter, softened | 75ml island gin |
| 225g golden caster sugar | *For the topping:* |
| 4 medium free-range eggs | 100g golden granulated sugar |
| 225g self-raising flour | Zest and juice of 1 lemon |
| 1 level tsp baking powder | 75ml island gin |
| Zest and juice of 1 lemon | A splash of tonic water |

Cream the butter and sugar well, until pale and fluffy, then beat in the eggs one at a time, adding a spoonful or so of the weighed flour with every egg to help prevent curdling.

Sift the remaining flour and baking powder together with a pinch of salt and gently fold this into the mix. Stir through the lemon zest and juice and the gin.

Tip into a prepared cake tin (a 20cm square cake tin, buttered and base-lined, leaving some lining paper overhanging so you can easily remove the cake from the tin. The cake tin must not be one with a removable base as in those tins the topping will not soak into the cake but seep through the base.)

Level the top and bake in a preheated oven (180C/350F/Gas 4) for 35 to 40 minutes until a wooden cocktail stick inserted into the middle comes out clean.

While the cake is baking, place the sugar in a wide jug and mix with the remaining ingredients. When the cake is ready, place on a board but do not remove from the tin. Prick all over the surface with a wooden cocktail stick and pour over the lemony gin syrup.

Allow to cool completely before removing carefully from the tin.

*Kiloran Bay, Colonsay.*

# WARM BERRY GIN COMPOTE WITH ROSE-PETAL ICE-CREAM

*serves 4–6*

*This ice-cream tastes exotic and perfumed, yet is seriously easy to make. All you need are a couple of scented roses (damask or other old-fashioned varieties are best), some cream, sugar and a dash of rosewater. Remember that most hothouse roses will have been sprayed, so avoid these at all costs. Pick garden roses soon after they have flowered and long before the petals fall off. Although all rose petals are edible, you should be guided by your nose: if the petals have a strong perfume, they will add plenty of alluring fragrance to your recipe. Choose either red or deep pink for the best visual effect.*

| For the ice-cream: | For the compote: |
|---|---|
| 2 scented, unsprayed roses | 125g raspberries |
| 425ml double cream | 125g black/redcurrants |
| 100g icing sugar, sifted | 125g blueberries |
| 2 tbsp natural yoghurt | 100ml gin |
| Rosewater | 50g caster sugar |
| | 125g strawberries |

For the ice-cream, remove the petals from the roses: very gently wash and rinse them if necessary. Trim off the bitter white part at the base of the petal. Place the petals in a heavy saucepan with the cream and bring slowly to the boil. When you see the bubbles, remove from the heat. Pour the contents into a bowl. When cold, place in the refrigerator for at least two hours, preferably overnight. Then strain the cream, reserving the petals.

Whip the cream with the icing sugar until it forms soft peaks. Stir in the yoghurt, and add rosewater to taste: 2 to 3 teaspoons should be enough, depending on its strength. Gently fold in the petals. Pour into a freezer container, seal and freeze for at least five hours or until solid – you don't even have to stir it. Serve with the warm compote.

For the compote, place the first five ingredients in a saucepan. Slowly heat until the sugar dissolves, then increase the heat and bubble for 1 minute. Remove from the heat and stir in the strawberries.

*Banna Minn beach, West Burra, Shetland.*

# Epilogue

My tour round the Scottish islands is over for now; but it has by no means come to an end. I only had time to visit some 20 of the hundreds of Scottish islands, from Luing in the south west of Scotland to Unst, the most northerly island in Shetland. But there is so much more: so many islands, so many more wonderful food stories.

I have delighted in speaking to producers of cheese and cured fish, farmers of beef and lamb and people fishing for ling, scallops and lobster. I have unearthed some wonderful old recipes, from Cormorant Soup on Great Bernera to Stewed Olick on the Out Skerries. Baking has featured strongly, with recipes for bannocks and oatcakes, cakes and dumpling. And though there are many regional variations, the basic concept is the same: a cloutie dumpling served on Tiree might differ slightly from the one made on Islay, but they both represent a taste of the past and a celebration of the present.

All over the islands, more cheeses are being made in the traditional way and the most exquisite honeys are being sealed in jars. And now gin distilleries are springing up, producing gin as the long wait for whisky to mature begins. These have their own unique flavours, depending on the variety of local botanicals, but all the island gins, from Jura to Harris, are keeping up with the zeitgeist and looking to both present trends and future tastes.

The islands are alive, they are vibrant. They are magnificent and haunting. They tug at the heartstrings and lure you back with an inexplicable attraction. Breathe in the beauty and splendour, the peacefulness and the charm. Meet the people, eat the food. But be warned: a taste of the Scottish islands will ruin you for life. You will be hooked. Start planning that trip now.